HOLIDAYS & CELEBRATIONS

WITH YOUR KIDS

Table of Contents

Table of Contents

Dear Kids,

Do you enjoy celebrating holidays? Your family probably celebrates some very special days in very special ways. There may be foods and sweets that you only eat on those holidays. Or maybe you go to visit friends and relatives. Or you may play games or take part in old family traditions and customs.

This book will give you ideas for activities, recipes, and projects for making all kinds of celebrations fun. There may be some holidays that you don't celebrate, and you don't really understand what they are all about. There may even be some celebrations that you've never heard of before!

There are popular holidays, days you might not have known were holidays, and holidays that are celebrated by other people around the world. Now you can celebrate, too!

When you are working on a project, look for these two things:

STOP When you see this, it means that step is a little challenging, and you will need an adult to help you.

This symbol means that it takes a little time to complete this activity—something may need to bake or dry—so be sure you have enough time to see it through.

To enjoy your celebrations the most, be sure you include your whole family.

Dear Mom & Dad,

Do you enjoy holidays mostly because of the time you spend with your children? Would you like to find a way to extend that joy and excitement all year long?

With this collection of fun holiday projects, you can discover new family customs and explore the traditions of others. These games, recipes, and crafts are easy and fun to do. And many can be enjoyed all year long, no matter what day it is!

To make it easier for you to choose an appropriate activity, each project and recipe is rated. At the top of the page, you will see one to four balloons. Here is what they mean:

These projects are easy. Your child could do them without your help.

These projects have more steps and use a number of skills. They may also use a stove or a knife. Your child will probably need your help.

These projects use a stove or a knife, so your child will probably need your help. Other than that, they are pretty easy.

These are the most challenging projects in the book. Your child will definitely need your help.

If your child is interested in an activity that is rated higher than you think he or she can understand, give it a try anyway. If your child is motivated and you are helping, no project is too hard! These activities will make special memories for you and your child.

So hang the paper streamers and start celebrating! Make the most of the time you spend together.

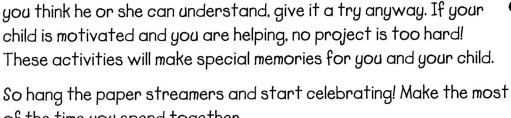

New Year's Celebrations
December 31 & January 1

In just about every country, people celebrate the New Year, although not always on January 1.

One popular way of getting ready for the coming year is to make new year's resolutions. These are promises you make to yourself to become a better person.

New Year's Eve is usually celebrated with big parties. People count down the seconds until the new year starts. At midnight, they blow horns and whistles. On New Year's Day, people march in and watch parades. Some people like to watch lots of football games.

One of the biggest New Year's Eve parties is in New York City's Times Square. Times Square is a place in the city where many streets meet. Thousands of people stand in the square on New Year's Eve. At midnight, they watch a big lighted ball drop down a pole on top of a building. You can watch this on television.

On New Year's Day, people often visit friends to start the new year off right. All over the world, people celebrate the new year in special ways.

In Greece, people bake *St. Basil's cakes.* Each cake has one coin baked inside. The person who gets the coin will have good luck in the coming year.

In Austria, children are given small toy pigs that carry good-luck coins or four-leaf clovers in their mouths.

In Japan, most people clean their houses to start off the new year!

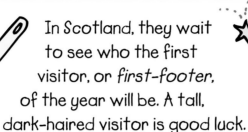

In Scotland, they wait to see who the first visitor, or *first-footer*, of the year will be. A tall, dark-haired visitor is good luck.

In Belgium, children write letters to their parents to wish them luck. Farmers wish a Happy New Year to their animals.

In the Bahamas, people march and dance in the Junkanoo parade while wearing colorful paper costumes.

In Denmark, people throw old pots and dishes at the doors of their friends' houses. They also play tricks like American children do on Halloween.

In France, people eat pancakes to bring themselves good luck.

In Puerto Rico, children throw pails of water out of windows at midnight. They believe this will get rid of the evil spirits that may be in their homes.

When the clock strikes midnight in Spain, people eat grapes—one grape for each time the clock strikes. Each grape brings good luck for one of the months in the year ahead.

New Year's celebrations don't just happen on January 1. The early Romans once celebrated the New Year on March 1. Early Christians would celebrate around March 25. Today, the Chinese, Muslims, and Jews all celebrate their New Year on other dates.

New Year Noisemakers

Blow these cardboard kazoos at midnight to ring in the New Year.

You'll need:

1 toilet tissue tube
glitter
ribbons
glue
crayons, markers, and paints
plastic wrap
scissors
rubber band
tape
pen

1. Use the crayons, markers, paints, glitter, and ribbons to decorate the tube.

2. With a pen, draw a 3-inch circle on the plastic wrap. STOP With help, cut out the circle.

3. Place the plastic circle over one end of the cardboard tube. Wrap a rubber band around the plastic to keep it in place.

4. To use your noisemaker, blow into the open end of the tube. Try humming, singing, and whooping.

Other noisemakers:

Place a handful of M&M's® on a paper plate. Fold the plate in half. Tape the edges of the plate together. Shake the noisemaker at midnight. Later break it open and enjoy the candy.

Rinse out an empty soda or juice can and let it dry. Drop in some dried beans or unpopped popcorn kernels. Cover the opening of the can with masking tape. Decorate the outside of the can. Shake the can to make noise.

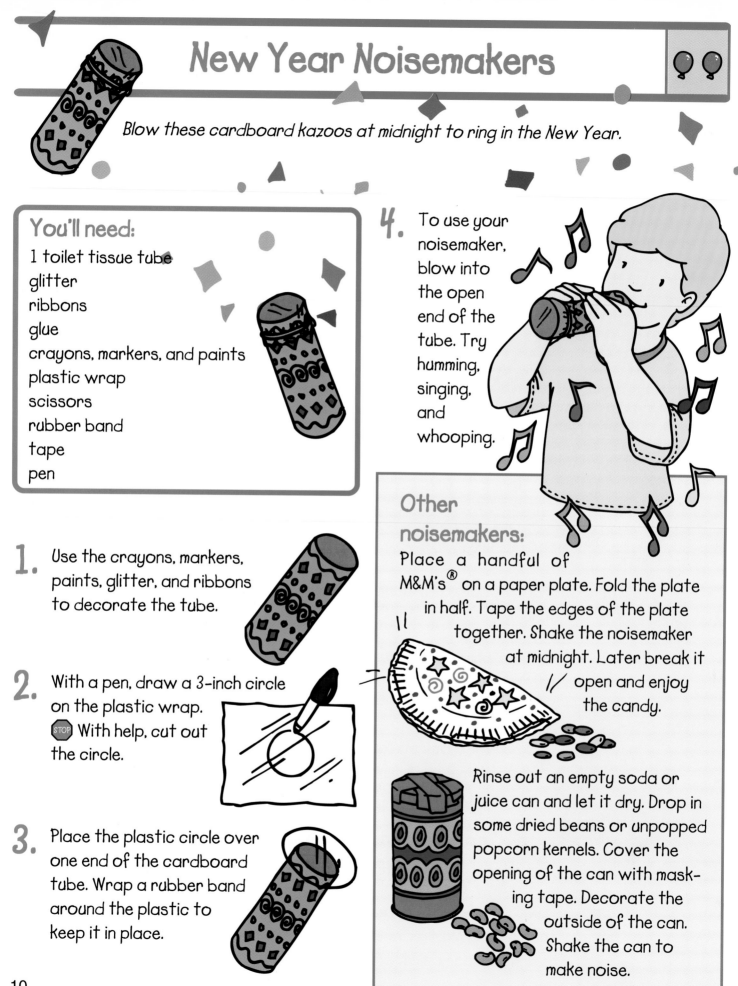

Time Capsule

Time capsules are a fun way to save special memories.

You'll need:

shoebox
paint
glue
glitter
markers
things you want to remember from the past year: photos, awards, newspaper clippings, ticket stubs, letters and postcards, party invitations, etc.

1. Decorate the shoebox with markers, paint, and glitter.

2. Ask everyone in your family to collect small things from the past year that have special memories.

3. Ask your family to sit in a circle with the box in the middle. Take turns telling everyone about one of your items, and put it in the box.

4. When you are finished, store the box under your bed or in a closet. Keep it there until the end of the year. At the end of the year, pull the box out and look through the memories you've collected there. Then start your next time capsule.

5. Throughout the year, save items that you want to put in your time capsule.

Handmade Calendar

Make this calendar to give as
a gift or to share with your family.

You'll need:

12 sheets of colored tagboard or
    construction paper, each
      11 inches by 17 inches
12 of your favorite photos (try to choose
    a photo that goes with each month of
    the year)
glue or tape
ruler
felt-tip markers
hole puncher
yarn or ribbon

2. Glue or tape one photo to the top of
each piece of paper. Under each photo
write the name of
the month it
represents. Use
each month only
once.

1. Be sure that the 12 photos you've
chosen are copies, not originals. Try to
match each picture with a certain
month—for example, a picture of you
opening your Christmas presents for
December, or a picture of Dad raking
leaves for October.

3. Use the markers and ruler to draw
a grid on the bottom of each piece of
paper. Each grid should be seven
squares across and five squares down,
as shown below. Above the grid, write in
the days of the
week, one day
over each column
of squares.
Start with
Sunday.

4. Look at a calendar for this year. What day of the week is December 31? The first of January will be the next day of the week. For example, if December 31 is on Monday, January 1 will be on Tuesday.

5. Write "1" in the upper left corner of the first Tuesday square (or whichever day of the week the year starts) on your January grid. Fill in the rest of the dates. Remember: April, June, September, and November have 30 days. February has 28 or 29—check a calendar for the coming year to find out which. The rest of the months have 31 days.

6. Write in special days on your calendar, like birthdays, anniversaries, the first day of school, Thanksgiving, Passover—any days that are important to your family.

7. Stack the pages in order by month, so January is at the top and December is at the bottom.

8. With a grown-up's help, punch two holes at the top of the calendar. String the ribbon or yarn through both holes and tie a bow in the front, as shown.

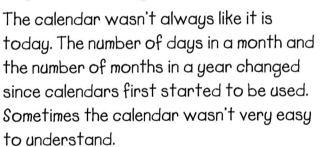

The calendar wasn't always like it is today. The number of days in a month and the number of months in a year changed since calendars first started to be used. Sometimes the calendar wasn't very easy to understand.

The Romans made mistakes when they planned their calendar. Around 46 B.C. their seasons were all confused! It was fall in July and winter in September.

Julius Caesar, a Roman general and leader, made some changes to the calendar. He even made the year 46 B.C. have 445 days. The Romans called this the *Year of Confusion.*

Hoppin' John

This traditional African-American dish is believed to bring you good luck if you eat it on New Year's Day.

Makes 3 to 4 servings

You'll need:

1/2 pound dried black-eyed peas
2 1/2 cups water
1/2 cup uncooked rice
1/2 pound lowfat sausage
1/2 medium onion, chopped
1/4 cup chopped celery
1 small garlic clove, minced
1/2 green bell pepper, seeded and chopped
1 can (10 ounces) chunky tomatoes
1/2 teaspoon salt
1/2 teaspoon ground black pepper

1. Soak the peas in water overnight.

2. Drain the peas into a colander. Run cold water over the peas. Take out any peas that are dried up, broken, or a weird color.

3. Place the peas and the 2 1/2 cups of water in a pot. (STOP) Ask a grown-up to bring the peas to a boil. Once they are boiling, turn the heat to low and let them simmer about 40 minutes.

4. (STOP) While you are waiting for the peas to cook, ask a grown-up to help you cook one cup of rice.

5. (STOP) With help, cut the sausage into 1/2-inch pieces. Ask your grown-up helper to brown the sausage in a nonstick skillet on low heat.

6. Add the onion, celery, garlic, and pepper to the skillet. (STOP) Cook for five more minutes.

7. Add the sausage mixture to the pot of peas. Add the salt, pepper, and tomatoes. Cover.

8. (STOP) Cook the Hoppin' John about 20 more minutes. Serve the mixture over the rice.

New Year's Bubbly

*Grown-ups like to ring in the New Year with some champagne.
Here's a tastier, "kid-rific" version for you and your friends.*

Makes 8 servings
You'll need:

12 ounces white grape juice
1 can frozen lemonade concentrate
1 package frozen strawberries, thawed
12 ounces 7-Up®
8 cherries or pineapple
   pieces

1. Place half of the first three ingredients in a blender. (STOP) Blend until smooth. Pour the mixture into a punch bowl or pitcher. Repeat with the remaining grape juice, lemonade concentrate, and strawberries.

2. Add the 7-Up® to the mixture. Stir.

3. Serve your bubbly in champagne glasses. Place a piece of fruit in each glass as you serve it.

Here are some of the wild tales people once believed about New Year's:

- Eat sauerkraut on New Year's Day for good health or wealth the whole year.
- If you eat a piece of herring at midnight, you will be lucky all year.
- If the salt shaker is full on New Year's Day, you will be lucky all year.
- If you cry on New Year's Day, you will be sad throughout the year.
- It is bad luck to sweep the house on New Year's Day.
- Animals kneel at midnight on New Year's Eve.

15

Chinese New Year
One Week Between January 21 and February 19

Chinese families celebrate the New Year after the harvest and before the next season's planting.

When families get ready for the New Year, they buy new clothes. They hope that these new clothes will disguise them so the evil spirits won't recognize them. Many people believe if they get haircuts during their preparations for the New Year, they will have good luck. Families also sweep and clean their homes, to be rid of the old luck and bring in the luck of the coming year. But once the New Year's celebration begins, Chinese families don't clean again until it's over; they are afraid they might sweep the new year's good luck out with the dust!

Homes are decorated with signs that say "Gung Hay Fat Choy!" (Happy New Year!) or "good luck" in Chinese. Poems are written out and hung on the walls. Lots of red is used for the decorations, because red is thought to be a lucky color. Oranges and red apples, symbols of luck, are stacked in pyramids on tables.

Some Chinese families believe the kitchen god Tsao-Chun is a spirit that lives in their homes. Before the New Year, Tsao-Chun flies to the heavens to report on whether the family has been good. On the night that Tsao-Chun leaves the house, the family will make a meal of sweet foods like fruit, honey, and sugar cane, to be sure the god says only sweet things about the family. Tsao-Chun comes back on New Year's Day.

On New Year's Eve, special foods are eaten, and some are left over to be eaten the next day. At midnight on New Year's Eve, fire-crackers are set off to welcome the kitchen god back.

On New Year's Day, everyone visits family and friends. Married people give red cloth envelopes with money inside to children and unmarried relatives. People only say and do kind things. They believe if they are good on New Year's Day, the rest of the year will be good to them.

The celebration goes on for seven days. At the end of the seven days, there is the Golden Dragon parade. The giant dragon puppet comes at the end of the parade, when fireworks are set off to scare away the evil spirits. Dragons were the symbol of the emperors of Japan, and stand for strength and goodness. The Dragon Parade is a way to wish everyone good luck for the coming year.

Chinese Riddle Lanterns

*During the first full moon of the New Year,
Chinese children march in a lantern parade.
Each lantern has a riddle attached to it for others to enjoy.*

You'll need:

two 1-inch by 6-inch strips of red,
    orange, or yellow paper
9-inch by 12-inch sheet of red, orange,
    or yellow construction paper
ruler
scissors
pencil
glue
stapler

1. Fold the construction paper in half lengthwise.

2. Hold the ruler so it is one inch from the long, open end. Trace along the edge of the ruler to make a line across the top of the paper, as shown.

3. Use the ruler to make lines about one inch apart down the length of the paper, as shown.

4. Hold the paper so the folded side is down and the open side is up. **STOP** With scissors, cut along the lines that are running up and down. Be sure to stop cutting when you reach the line that runs across the top.

5. Unfold the paper. **STOP** Roll the paper and staple the ends together, as shown.

6. Glue a paper strip to the top of the lantern to make a handle.

7. Think of a riddle, and write it on the other paper strip. Glue one end of the strip to the bottom of the lantern so the strip hangs from the lantern, as shown.

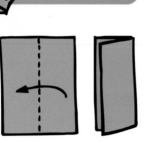

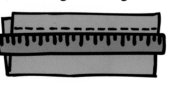

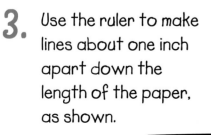

What has four legs and wings?

New Year Pudding Cake (Ting-shêng-kao)

Pudding cake is often given as a gift during the Chinese New Year festivities. This recipe is most popular in southern China.

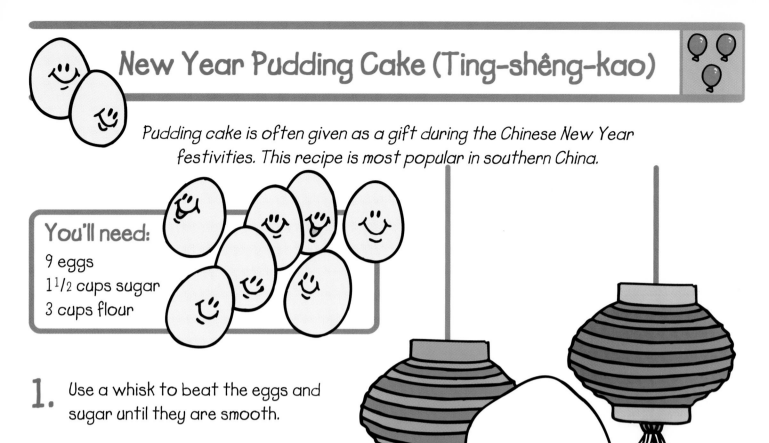

You'll need:

9 eggs
1 1/2 cups sugar
3 cups flour

1. Use a whisk to beat the eggs and sugar until they are smooth.

2. Add the flour to the mixture, a few tablespoons at a time. Each time you add a little, whisk the mixture again.

3. Run butter along the inside bottom and sides of a 9-inch cake pan. Pour the cake mix into the pan.

4. Pour 1 1/2 inches of water in a large skillet. Place the cake pan in the skillet. Cover the skillet. **STOP** Ask a grown-up to bring the water to a boil. Reduce the heat and simmer for 30 minutes, or until the cake is set in the middle.

5. Chill the cake in the refrigerator. Cut into pieces and serve.

Wontons

Try eating your wontons with chopsticks.

You'll need:

1 1/2 cups finely chopped cooked chicken
2 tablespoons finely chopped celery
1 tablespoon soy sauce
3 dozen wonton skins
cooking oil

1. Combine the chicken, celery, and soy sauce in a bowl.

2. Place the wonton skins on waxed paper. Put a rounded teaspoon of the chicken mixture in the center of each wonton.

3. Dip your index finger in water and run it along the edges of a wonton skin. Fold the wonton in half diagonally to make a triangle-shaped pouch. Press down on the edges to seal the wonton. Pull the bottom corners toward each other and pinch them together. Do this with the rest of the chicken mixture and wonton skins.

4. (STOP) Ask a grown-up to fry the wontons in about 1/2 inch of cooking oil until they are light brown. Drain the wontons on paper towels and let them cool.

Using chopsticks

1. Place the lower chopstick in the crook of your thumb beside the pointer finger. Let it rest against your middle finger.

2. Place the other chopstick between your pointer finger and your thumb.

3. Keep the lower chopstick still, and move the upper chopstick with your thumb and middle fingers to pick up the wonton.

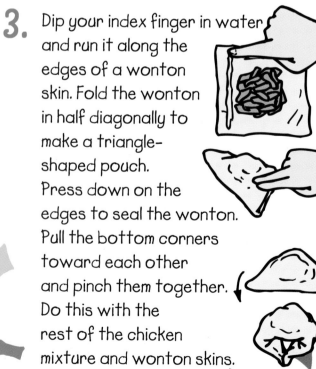

Fortune Cookies

Fortune cookies are a fun way to discover what the year ahead holds for you.

Makes 16

You'll need:

1/2 cup cake flour
1/4 cup sugar
2 tablespoons cornstarch
dash of salt
1/4 cup oil
2 egg whites
2 tablespoons water
sixteen 1/2-inch by 2-inch strips of paper
cooking spray

Cookies must be made one at a time.

1. Write a prediction or good luck wish on each strip of paper.

A joyous life will be yours.

2. Combine the flour, sugar, cornstarch, and salt. Add the oil and the egg whites. Stir until the mixture is smooth.

3. Add water. Stir until it is mixed well.

4. Spray a small amount of cooking spray into a frying pan. (STOP) Ask a grown-up to heat the pan . Pour about a tablespoon of the batter into the frying pan, and quickly spread it into a circle. Cook over low heat for about four minutes, until it is lightly brown. Flip the cookie over and let it cook for one more minute, until that side is slightly brown.

5. (STOP) Ask your helper to remove the cookie from the pan and place it on a towel or potholder.

6. Place a fortune in the center of the cookie. Holding the potholder, fold the cookie in half, as shown below.

7. Bend the cookie into a half-moon shape. Place the cookie in one section of a muffin tin to cool.

8. Repeat steps 4 through 7 until all the cookies are made.

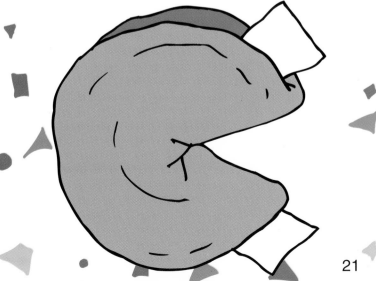

21

Dr. Martin Luther King, Jr. Day
The Third Monday in January

Dr. Martin Luther King, Jr., was a leader of the civil rights movement. He wanted everyone to see that all people were equal and should be treated the same.

He was born in Atlanta, Georgia, on January 15, 1929. When Martin was a boy, there were many unfair laws. Black children and white children could not go to the same school. Black people could not eat in restaurants where white people ate. They could not use the same parks, bathrooms, or water fountains. Separating people because they have different colors of skin is *segregation*.

Martin was very smart. He skipped the 9th and 12th grades. He started at Morehouse College when he was only 15 years old. He wanted to be a minister and became a doctor of theology. He married Coretta Scott and moved to Montgomery, Alabama. There Dr. King was the pastor at the Dexter Avenue Baptist Church.

On December 1, 1955, a black woman named Rosa Parks was taking the bus home from work in Montgomery, Alabama. The bus became crowded, and the bus driver told Rosa to give her seat to a white rider. The tired Rosa would not get up. The bus driver had her arrested.

Dr. King and other people in the community were very upset and asked all the black people to stop taking buses until the laws were changed. This is called a *boycott*.

Dr. King believed that people should not be violent when they wanted to change something. He believed in peaceful marches and demonstrations. The bus boycott worked. The *U.S. Supreme Court* said that black people should be able to sit anywhere on a bus.

After the boycott, Dr. King and other ministers started a group called the Southern Christian Leadership Conference. This group wanted to change unfair laws. Dr. King led many marches and was sometimes put in jail.

Dr. King's most famous march was the March on Washington on August 28, 1963. He was joined by 250,000 people! On the steps of the Lincoln Memorial, he gave his famous "I Have a Dream" speech. Here is a little bit of it:

> "I have a dream that my four little children will one day live in a nation where they will not be judged by the color of their skin but by the content of their character."

In 1964, Dr. King won the Nobel Peace Prize, which is awarded every year to the person who has done the most to bring peace to the world.

Dr. King also tried to help the poor. In 1968, he went to Memphis, Tennessee, to help garbage workers get better pay. On April 4, as he walked out of his hotel room, he was shot. He died a little while later. He was buried in Atlanta. On his gravestone these words are written:

> "Free at last. Free at last. Thank God Almighty, I'm free at last."

Dr. King's work helped to change many unfair segregation laws. He also helped black people get equal voting power.

Today, his birthday is celebrated as a national holiday in the United States. It is a time to remember what he did, and what he wanted all of us to do to make the world a better place.

Friendship Bracelet

Wear this bracelet all year long to remember this important day.

You'll need:

black beads
white beads
red heart-shaped beads
glue
yarn

2. String the beads onto the yarn.

3. Tie a knot with the ends of the yarn.

1. Dip each end of the yarn into the glue. Let it dry overnight.

Peace Wreath

Hang this wreath on a door or a wall to celebrate Martin Luther King's birthday. It's so pretty, you may want to keep it up all year long.

You'll need:

1 piece poster board
black, white, brown, red, and
   yellow construction paper
pencil
glue
scissors
red, white, and black
   ribbons

3. Glue the hands onto the wreath shape, so they overlap (see below).

4. Holding the three pieces of ribbon together, make a bow. Glue the bow to the bottom of your wreath.

1. Draw a large circle on the poster board. **STOP** With help, cut out the circle. Then cut out the center of the circle to make a wreath shape.

2. Trace your hand onto a piece of construction paper. **STOP** With help, cut out the hand shape. Continue making hand shapes, until you have enough hands to cover the wreath.

Groundhog Day
February 2

On Groundhog Day, people want to know if spring will be starting soon. They wait for a groundhog to come out of its den. If the groundhog sees its shadow and runs back in the den, there will be six more weeks of winter. If it doesn't see its shadow and stays outside, spring is coming.

This custom started in Europe where farmers would look for bears, badgers, and other animals to come out of their dens. When the Germans came to the United States to settle in Pennsylvania, they brought this idea with them. For a long time, people have believed that when animals wake from their long winter's nap, springtime must be coming.

Groundhogs, which are also called woodchucks, are about two feet long from their heads to their bushy tails. They have grayish-brown fur. They dig underground dens that have many "rooms" and more than one entrance. Groundhogs *hibernate* (sleep) during the winter. When they leave their dens to look for food, they sit up on their hind legs and look around for any signs of danger.

Shadow Tag

Play with your own shadow on Groundhog Day.

You'll need:

at least one other player

1. Go outside on a sunny day.

2. One person is It.

3. It tries to step on the shadow of one of the other players. When she does, the player whose shadow she stepped on becomes It.

Figure it out: Is it easier to step on shadows at certain times of the day?

Valentine's Day
February 14

Valentine's Day is a special time when we tell people that we love them and care about them. There are many stories about the beginning of Valentine's Day.

One story says that a long time ago, in early Rome, there was a priest named Valentine. Claudius II, who was emperor at the time, made a law that no one could become engaged or get married. He was afraid if men had sweethearts or wives, they would not want to fight in wars. But Valentine felt sorry for the young people who were in love. So he married them secretly. When Emperor Claudius found out, he had Valentine put to death. Some say this happened on February 14.

Another story is about another man named Valentine. He also lived in Rome when Claudius II was emperor. He was put in jail because he was helping Christians, people who Claudius didn't like. Valentine became very friendly with the jailer's blind daughter. When he was beheaded on February 14, he sent her a message that said, "From your Valentine."

But February 14 was also the time for a special Roman celebration called Lupercalia. Romans hoped it would bring them good crops and keep their animals safe.

Valentine's Day probably has a little bit of history from all these stories.

To celebrate the day today, people send special cards with romantic messages. They give their sweethearts little gifts and tokens. One story says that the first valentine was written in the 1400s by Duke Charles of Orleans. He was French and he was captured by the English during a war. While he sat in his prison, he wrote poems for his wife. In one of them, he mentioned Valentine and Cupid. Over time, hearts, cupids, flowers, and pairs of birds have come to symbolize the holiday, and these are often found on valentine cards.

Sweet Heart Cookies

Make these yummy treats for your valentine.

You'll need:

1/3 cup butter
1/4 cup honey
2/3 cup oats
1/3 cup nonfat dry milk
4 teaspoons water
3/4 cup flour
1 teaspoon baking powder
1/4 teaspoon salt

1. **STOP** With help, mix together the butter and honey.

2. Add the oats, dry milk, and water. Mix well.

3. Add the flour, baking powder, and salt. Mix well. The dough should be soft.

4. Use a rolling pin to roll out the dough. It should be 1/4- to 1/2-inch thick.

5. Use a heart-shaped cookie cutter to cut out the cookies.

6. **STOP** Ask a grown-up to bake the cookies for 10 to 15 minutes in a 325° oven.

Heartfelt Valentines

These oversized valentines are made with an extra-big dose of love.

You'll need:

1 sheet 8½-inch by 11-inch paper
pencil
scissors
poster board, at least 16 inches by 22 inches
2 small pieces of sponge
2 colors of paint (pink and red would be nice)
glitter
hole puncher
ribbon
1 brad fastener

1. On the 8½-inch by 11-inch paper, draw a big heart. (STOP) Cut it out.

2. Trace the heart twice on the poster board to make two heart shapes. (STOP) Cut out both hearts.

3. In the middle of one of the hearts, draw a smaller heart, as shown below.

4. Dip a sponge in some paint, and sponge-paint the inside heart. While the paint is still wet, sprinkle on some glitter.

5. Using a different color of paint, sponge-paint the heart-shaped border. Let the paint dry.

6. 🛑 With help, punch holes about one inch apart around the outline of the smaller heart, as shown below.

7. Lace the ribbon in and out of the holes. Start at the top and finish at the top, tying the ends into a bow.

8. On the second heart, write a message to your valentine. Place the painted heart on top of the message heart. Push a brad fastener through the top of both hearts to hold them together.

message inside

Will you be my Valentine? Happy Valentine's Day

During the 1890s, many valentines were shaped like or showed drawings of tomatoes! At the time, tomatoes were grown as flowers and were not eaten. They were considered beautiful and were called love apples. They were the perfect symbol for a special valentine!

Mardi Gras
The Two Weeks Before Ash Wednesday

Mardi Gras celebrations take place two weeks before the serious time of Lent begins.

In French, *Mardi gras* means "fat Tuesday." The name may have come from an old custom of parading a fat ox through the streets on Shrove Tuesday, the day before Ash Wednesday. Or, it could come from all the eating people do on that day!

Mardi Gras is celebrated around the world. There are Mardi Gras festivals in Italy, Brazil, Germany, France, and other countries around the world.

The holiday came to America with the French settlers. The most famous Mardi Gras party in the United States is in New Orleans, Louisiana. All kinds of parades, parties, and balls go on during two weeks of Mardi Gras. The parades have bands, performers, and big floats. The people in the parades wear fancy costumes and masks. So do some of the people watching the parade! The people, floats, and streets are covered in purple, green, and gold. These are the official colors of Mardi Gras.

The people that ride on the floats throw strings of beads, fake gold coins called *doubloons*, and little trinkets to the people that are watching. Some people bring ladders to the parades that have special seats built on top. This is where the children sit so they can see better and catch more stuff. If you were watching the parade and wanted someone to throw you something, you'd catch their eye and yell, "Throw me something, mister!"

Each parade has a king, or a *rex*, and there is also a rex for the whole Mardi Gras celebration. These kings are chosen by the groups that put on the parades, which are called *krewes*. The rex sits on his throne on a special float during his parade.

There is always lots of *yummy* food at Mardi Gras. One traditional treat that you can only get during this carnival time is a king cake. A king cake is shaped like a ring, and is twisted so it looks like it is braided. There is icing on top along with purple, green, and yellow sugar crystals. Inside the king cake, the baker puts a tiny doll. If you get the piece with the doll, you are king for a day. You also *must* bring a king cake to the next party.

Pancakes

Stack up some pancakes to celebrate Shrove Tuesday.

You'll need:

2 tablespoons butter
1/4 cup all-purpose flour
1/4 cup whole wheat flour
3/4 teaspoon baking powder
1/4 teaspoon sugar
1/8 teaspoon salt
1/2 beaten egg
1/2 cup milk
pancake toppings such as syrup, jam,
    whipped cream, fruit

1. **STOP** Ask a grown-up to heat one tablespoon of butter in a frying pan over medium heat (or melt it in a microwave). Once the butter is melted, take the pan off the stove.

2. Combine the flours, baking powder, sugar, and salt in a large bowl.

3. Whisk together the egg, melted butter, and milk. Pour this mixture into the flour mix. Whisk together until the batter is smooth.

4. **STOP** Ask your grown-up helper to melt 1/2 tablespoon of butter in a frying pan. Be sure the butter covers the bottom of the pan.

5. **STOP** Spoon the batter by tablespoonfuls into the frying pan. When the batter starts to bubble (about two minutes), check the bottom of the pancake to see if it is brown. If so, flip the pancake over and cook the pancake about two minutes more.

6. You need to melt butter in the pan for each group of pancakes you make. You can serve your pancakes with maple syrup, jam, whipped cream, fruit, honey, applesauce, or anything else you think will make them taste yummy.

In Great Britain, Mardi Gras Day is called Shrove Tuesday or Pancake Day. In one town in England over 500 years ago, a woman was flipping her pancakes when she heard the church bells ring. When she realized she was late for church, she took off running. She was in such a hurry, she forgot to put down her skillet. This turned into a traditional pancake race that is run every year. The women run with their skillets full of pancakes and the first to reach the church gets a kiss from the bell ringer.

34

Miniature King Cakes

Here is an easy version of the popular Mardi Gras treat.

Serves 2

You'll need:

1 large can of cinnamon rolls
vanilla icing
yellow, green, and purple
    sprinkles or sugar
    crystals

1. Unroll the cinnamon-roll dough. Make two separate strips.

2. Braid the strips of dough together, as shown below. Form an oval with the braid and press the edges together.

3. 🛑 Bake the dough according to the directions on the package.

4. When the dough is cool, spread the icing on the top of the cake. Sprinkle the sugar or sprinkles on the cake.

Mardi Gras Masks

People love to wear fancy costumes and masks during Mardi Gras.

You'll need:

cardboard or poster board
pencil
X-acto® knife
hole puncher
sequins, beads, glitter
glue
marker, crayons, or paints
Popsicle® stick
6 feet of curling ribbon,
    cut in 2-foot lengths
scissors

1. On the cardboard draw a shape for the mask. (Some ideas are shown below.)

2. 🛑 Cut out the mask shape. Hold it up to your face. Draw in the eyes.
🛑 Ask a grown-up to cut out the eyes with the X-acto® knife.

3. 🛑 Punch a hole in one side of the mask. Decorate the mask with the sequins, beads, glitter, markers, and paints. Also decorate the Popsicle® stick.

4. Glue the Popsicle® stick to the back of the mask, on the side with the hole as shown.

5. Thread the three lengths of ribbon through the hole. Pull each ribbon through the hole until there is an even amount hanging from each side of the hole. Knot the ribbons to keep them in place.

6. 🛑 Ask a grown-up to curl the ribbons for you, using scissors.

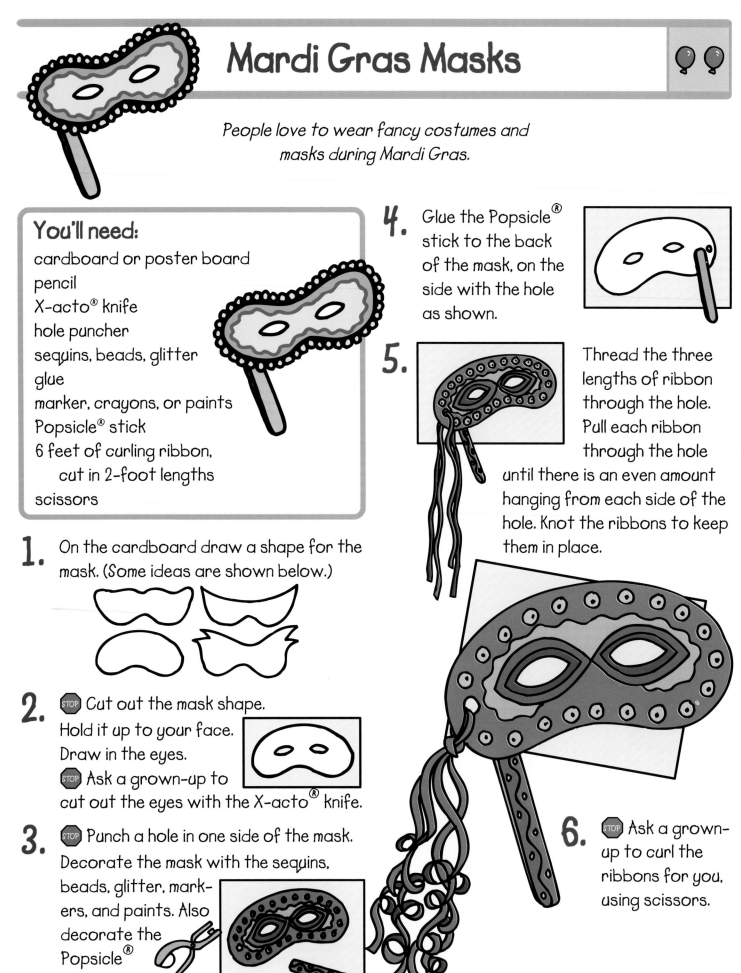

36

Presidents' Day
Third Monday in February

Presidents' Day celebrates the birthdays of George Washington and Abraham Lincoln. It is a federal holiday, which means it is celebrated across the country. It also means that the post office does not deliver mail, and schools, banks, and government offices are all closed.

George Washington was the first president of the United States. He was born in Virginia on February 22, 1732.

When the American colonists decided it was time to fight the British for their freedom, Washington was put in charge of the armies. It was a tough job. The soldiers often did not have enough food, weapons, clothing, or shelter, especially in the winter. Because Washington suffered right along with his men, the colonists respected him and began to look up to him.

When the war was over, some people wanted Washington to become king, but he didn't think that was a good idea. A few years later in 1789, Washington was elected president of the new country. George Washington is considered one of our most important presidents, because he helped set up the new government. He is called the Father of Our Country.

Abraham Lincoln was our 16th president. He was born on February 12, 1809, in Kentucky. Before he became president, he had been a soldier, postmaster, state legislator, congressman, and lawyer.

Lincoln led the country through the Civil War. He worked hard to make sure that the United States stayed as one country instead of breaking up into smaller nations. He also ended slavery. His actions throughout the war made him one of the most respected leaders in the world, even today.

Lincoln was reelected for another four years in the White House. But on April 14, 1865, he was shot by John Wilkes Booth at Ford's Theatre in Washington. He died the next day.

Presidents' Day is a good day to honor all the men who have served as the President of the United States.

Pretzel Log Cabin

President Abraham Lincoln was born in a log cabin, so celebrate his birthday by building a miniature version that you can eat.

You'll need:

Straight pretzels
peanut butter
empty pint-size milk carton,
    washed and dried
glue
butter knife or spatula

1. Glue the milk carton shut. Let it dry.

2. Using a butter knife, spread the peanut butter over the whole milk carton (except the bottom).

3. Stick the pretzels to the peanut butter to make a log cabin. Make the door and windows first. To make the door, stick several pretzels lengthwise in the middle of one of the walls as shown. To make a window, just use the pretzel sticks to make the outline of the window, as shown.

4. Lay the pretzel sticks across the four walls and lengthwise on the roof. Bite off the ends of the pretzels to make them fit.

5. Use your cabin as a decoration, but don't forget to eat the pretzels and peanut butter before it dries out.

Easy Cherry Tarts

Legends say that George Washington cut down a cherry tree when he was a little boy. This probably isn't true, but cherries are still sometimes used as a symbol for this holiday.

You'll need:

1 can of refrigerated biscuits

cherry pie filling

4. 🛑 Bake the biscuits according to the directions on the can.

1. Use your hands to flatten each biscuit in the package. Place the flattened biscuits on a baking sheet.

2. Place a spoonful of cherry pie filling in the center of each biscuit.

3. Fold the biscuit in half. Press a fork around the edges of the biscuit to keep it together (see below).

St. Patrick's Day
March 17

Saint Patrick is the patron saint of Ireland. That means he watches over the Irish people and keeps them safe. This holiday celebrates his life.

Saint Patrick was born in England. When he was 16, he was kidnapped by pirates and became the slave of an Irish chief. After six years, he escaped and returned to England. He decided he wanted to help the Irish tribes learn about God, so he studied religion in a *monastery*. Then he went back to Ireland. In Ireland, he started more than 300 churches and baptized more than 120,000 people!

St. Patrick's Day is a national holiday in Ireland. It is also a religious holiday—people go to special religious services and visit family and friends.

The first St. Patrick's celebration in the United States took place in Boston in 1737. Today the largest St. Patrick's Day parade is held in New York City. In the United States, the holiday is really a celebration of being Irish.

People march in parades and wear green to show that they are proud to be Irish. In New York City, the Empire State Building is lit with green lights on St. Patrick's Day. And in Chicago, Illinois, and San Antonio, Texas, the people color the water in their rivers green!

Many families in the United States eat special Irish foods on St. Patrick's Day. Corned beef and cabbage, mulligatawny soup, and Irish soda bread are favorite foods. Many dishes contain potatoes.

Shamrocks have become the symbol for this holiday because legends say Saint Patrick used shamrocks to help teach about God. He told the Irish people that God was made up of three parts, just like a shamrock.

There are many other symbols, too. Harps have played the music of Ireland for as long as anyone can remember. Leprechauns are a part of the many legends that the Irish tell about fairies and other "wee ones," as they call them. Clay pipes, the Irish flag, and bagpipes are also used to decorate banners on this day.

Potato Cakes

Potatoes have long been an important part of Irish meals.

You'll need:

1/4 cup butter
3/4 cup white flour
1/2 teaspoon salt
1/2 teaspoon baking powder
3 cups freshly mashed potatoes (with milk)
waxed paper

1. Place the flour in a bowl. (STOP) Ask a grown-up to cut the butter into the flour until it looks like large peas.

2. Add the salt and baking powder. Mix well.

3. Mix in the potatoes. Knead the mixture together for a few minutes.

4. Spread a light covering of flour on a table covered with waxed paper or on a cutting board. With help, roll out the mixture with a floured rolling pin.

5. (STOP) Cut the mixture into four rounds. Cook in a lightly buttered skillet until brown on both sides. Serve hot.

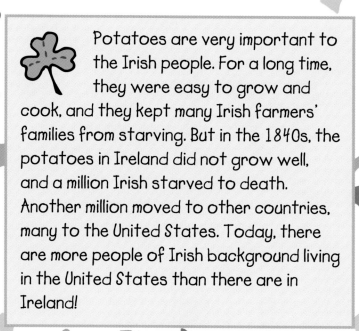

Potatoes are very important to the Irish people. For a long time, they were easy to grow and cook, and they kept many Irish farmers' families from starving. But in the 1840s, the potatoes in Ireland did not grow well, and a million Irish starved to death. Another million moved to other countries, many to the United States. Today, there are more people of Irish background living in the United States than there are in Ireland!

42

Soda Farls

*Soda farls and soda breads are
popular bakery treats in Ireland.*

You'll need:

1 cup all-purpose flour
1 cup cake flour
2 teaspoons baking soda
1 teaspoon salt
1 cup buttermilk

1. Mix the flours, baking soda, and salt.

2. Add the buttermilk. Stir until it becomes doughy.

3. Knead the dough gently on a floured cutting board.

4. Make a 10-inch circle with half the dough. Make a second circle with the rest of the dough.

5. Cut each circle into quarters.

6. **STOP** Ask a grown-up to fry each farl in a little bit of butter until it is browned (about five to seven minutes on each side). You may need to set each farl on end to help cook the sides.

The smallest park in America was built in Portland, Oregon, on St. Patrick's Day. It covers 452 inches and was built for leprechauns and snail races.

Irish Harp Mobile

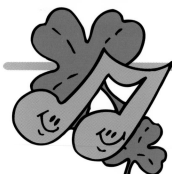

Hang this harp decoration in your house to welcome St. Patrick's Day.

You'll need:

white poster board
pencil
scissors
gold and green paint
paintbrush
hole puncher
green yarn
tape
glue
2 chopsticks

3. **STOP** Cut out four shamrocks like the one below from the poster board. Paint the shamrocks green. Let them dry.

4. Glue the shamrocks to the harps as shown.

1. Draw a harp shape like the one below on the poster board. Draw three more. **STOP** With help, cut out the shapes.

2. Paint the harps gold. Let them dry.

5. **STOP** Ask a grown-up to punch five holes at the top of each harp, and five holes at the bottom of each, as shown.

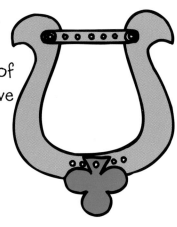

44

6. Weave a length of yarn into and out of the holes in each harp to make the harp strings, as shown. Tape the yarn ends to the back of each harp.

7. Hold the chopsticks together so they make a cross. Wrap yarn around the point where they cross to hold them together. Wrap the yarn around one way and then the other, so they stay evenly spaced. Wrap a length of string around the center of the chopsticks and tie the ends to make a hanger.

8. STOP Ask a grown-up to punch a hole at the top of each harp. Thread a length of string through each hole. Tie one end of each string around the hole in each harp, and the other end of each string around one end of each chopstick.

9. Hang your mobile using the hanger at the top.

A.

B.

C.

D.

April Fools' Day
April 1

In many countries, people celebrate April Fools' Day by playing jokes on others. One of the most popular tricks is sending someone to find something that doesn't exist. Many other people celebrate the holiday by making it a "backwards" day.

They wear their clothes inside out and backwards, walk backwards, eat breakfast for dinner, and wear their socks over their shoes.

Some people that study history think that April Fools' Day started in France. Up until the mid-1500s, the New Year was celebrated from March 25 to April 1. On April 1, everyone would exchange gifts. But in the 1560s, King Charles IX changed New Year's Day to January 1. Some people were stubborn, though, and still celebrated the New Year on April 1. People would make fun of them. People who celebrated the New Year in April were called April fish and sent joke gifts.

46

Breakfast Dinner

Here's a fun, but delicious, trick to play on your family!

You'll need:

breakfast foods like muffins, bagels, toast, donuts

breakfast drinks like milk, juice, tea, and coffee

dishes and silverware to set the table

1. Ask a grown-up in the house if you can make "dinner" for the rest of the family on April 1. Tell your helper you are actually going to serve breakfast food.

2. Ask the grown-up to help you collect the ingredients.

3. Announce to your family that you will be making dinner for everyone on that day.

4. With your grown-up helper, prepare the food for the meal.

5. Set the table.

6. Surprise your family with breakfast foods for dinner!

7. Be sure to yell, "Happy April Fools' Day!"

... toast, fried eggs, blueberry muffins, sausage links, orange juice, and ...

Fun Fact:

Eating breakfast for dinner, wearing your clothes inside out, and playing a trick on someone are all ways to celebrate April Fools' Day. Some people even try to walk backwards all day, but that is really hard.

Plennie Wingo walked backwards from Santa Monica, California, to Istanbul, Turkey, between April 15, 1931 and October 24, 1932. That's a total of 8,000 miles—no joke!

Passover
A Week During Late March or Mid-April

A long time ago, the Israelites were slaves for the Egyptians. One night in spring over 3,000 years ago, they escaped. Jewish people all over the world celebrate this special occasion at Passover.

On Passover, which is called *Pesach* in Hebrew, families take part in the *seder*. A seder is a dinner that includes singing, storytelling, and special foods. This dinner reminds everyone of the slavery of their Jewish ancestors and the freedom they found.

To get ready for Passover, families clean their houses, clean food out of their refrigerators, and even unpack special plates that are only used during Passover.

The Seder is read from a book called a *Haggadah*. It leads the family through 15 steps that retell the story of how the Jews became free. These steps include the youngest child asking four questions, a door being opened to welcome the prophet Elijah, leaving an empty chair at the table for Elijah, and finding a hidden piece of *matzo* (a flat bread made without yeast).

The food served at the seder is very symbolic. There is a large plate that sits in front of the leader of the seder. On that plate there are bits of a white root, *haroset*, a piece of lamb bone, a roasted egg, a piece of matzo, and fresh greens.

The bits of white root are called *maror*. They are bitter herbs, to remind the family of the bitterness of Egyptian slavery.

Haroset is a mixture of apples, nuts, and cinnamon. It is sweet because the Jews believed in the promise of a better life.

The lamb bone, which is called a *z'roah*, sits next to the haroset on the plate. It reminds everyone of the lamb that the Jews ate quickly right before they ran away from Egypt.

Next to the bone is the roasted egg. It is called the *beitzah* and stands for the animal sacrifices that were brought to the Temple for each festival.

The greens on the plate are usually parsley or lettuce. They stand for new life. They are dipped in saltwater before they are eaten. The saltwater stands for the tears cried by the slaves.

Matzo is also served at the seder. When the Israelites were hurrying to leave Egypt, they didn't have time to let their bread rise. So it did not get big and fluffy like the bread you buy in the store. Matzo is eaten at a seder to remind the family of this.

The word *Passover* comes from a story in the Bible about the tenth plague. God was angry with the Egyptians because they kept the Israelites as slaves. God killed the oldest child in every Egyptian family, but passed over the houses of the Israelites.

Haroset

This yummy spread represents the material the Jewish people used to build pyramids when they were slaves.

You'll need:

1 cup chopped apples
1/2 cup chopped walnuts
2 teaspoons cinnamon
1 teaspoon honey
1 tablespoon grape juice
matzos

2. Serve with matzos.

1. Mix together all the ingredients except the matzos. Let the mixture sit for a little while.

HONEY

CINN

GRAPE JUI

Passover Polo

Most of the Passover games include nuts!

3 or more players

You'll need:

big bag of peanuts (with the shells on)
masking tape

1. With the masking tape, make a small circle or square on the floor.

2. Choose someone to play the banker. Each player gets five nuts. The banker holds the bag of nuts.

3. Taking turns, throw a handful of nuts at the circle or square. You may throw as many of your nuts as you wish, but they must all be thrown at one time.

4. If you get an even number of nuts in the circle or square, the banker gives the player that many nuts from the peanut bank. The player also takes back all of her original nuts.

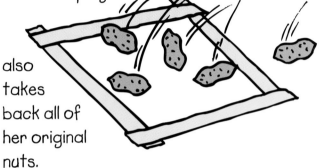

5. If an odd number of nuts lands in the circle, the player gets no nuts. All nuts that fall outside the circle go to the banker.

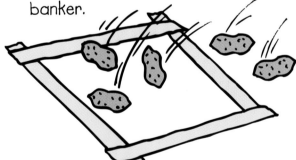

6. Play until the peanut bank is empty, or for a set number of rounds. The player with the most peanuts at the end of the game is the winner.

Passover Golf

Here's another nut game!

2 or more players

You'll need:

construction paper
scissors
masking tape
one peanut for
 each player
paper
pencil

1. Draw 9 to 18 circles or squares on the construction paper. Make them three to five inches across (the larger they are, the easier the game will be). 🛑 Cut out the shapes.

2. Tape the shapes to the floor. These are your golf "holes." Make sure there is some space between each shape. Scatter them throughout the house. Try putting them in funny places, like behind furniture or in a cup.

3. Decide how far away from each hole to stand or kneel when you are playing.

4. Taking turns for each hole, flick your peanut with your fingers to try and get it on top of the shape. Count how many flicks it takes for you to do this. That is your score for the hole. Write that number down.

5. Keep track of the scores for all players for each hole. Add up each player's score at the end. The player with the least number of points is the winner.

Easter

Easter is the most important holiday for Christians around the world. They believe that on this day, Jesus rose from the dead after he was crucified. They believe that they will also have life after death, in heaven.

A long time ago before people celebrated Easter, they often celebrated springtime with a festival. Once Easter began, the two holidays sometimes mixed together. That's because they both celebrate new life. Easter honors the new life of Jesus, and spring reminds us of the new life of the flowers, animals, and plants of the earth.

One custom of the spring festival that is now a part of Easter is decorating eggs. During the festival, people gave eggs as gifts to one another. An egg is a symbol of new life. When the shell cracks, new life is born.

Bunnies were also a symbol of the old spring festival. Bunnies have lots of babies, so they are another symbol of new life.

Many people go to special church services on Easter Sunday. Sometimes the church services are early in the morning, at sunrise. Families often wear new clothes on this holiday and walk in Easter parades after church to show them off. A long time ago, people were often baptized on Easter Sunday. They wore new white clothes to celebrate. This custom may be why people still like to get new Easter outfits today.

Many children get baskets of candy and toys from the Easter Bunny, and take part in egg hunts and egg rolls.

Make Your Own Egg Dye

Try mixing up these colors using ingredients found in your own house to dye hard-boiled eggs with.

Pink Dye:
Pour cranberry juice into a large bowl. Place the eggs you want to make pink in the bowl. Let them soak for awhile.

Red Dye:
With help, take some of the outside skins from a few red onions. Put the skins in a saucepan and add two cups of water. STOP Ask a grown-up to boil the water with the eggs you want to color for about 45 minutes.

Light Pink Dye:
Buy some fresh cranberries. Rub the berries over the eggs.

Yellow Dye:
Mix together 2/3 cup hot water, 1/4 teaspoon vinegar, and 1 teaspoon turmeric. Dip the eggs into the mixture.

Brown Dye:
Mix together 2/3 cup hot water and 1/2 teaspoon vinegar. Add one tablespoon of instant coffee and stir until the coffee dissolves in the liquid. Soak the eggs in the liquid.

Light Blue Dye:
Rub fresh blueberries over the eggs you want to make light blue.

Try experimenting with different berries, fruits, and flowers to dye eggs other colors.

Tie-Dye Eggs

*These colorful eggs will add flair
to your Easter egg hunt.*

You'll need:

hard-boiled eggs
food coloring
plastic cups
vinegar
eyedropper
cloth scraps, big enough to wrap around
    an egg

1. Cover the table with newspaper.

2. For each color—put two tablespoons of water in a cup. Add the colors of food coloring you want the dye to be. Use the eyedropper to add three drops of vinegar.

3. Wet a piece of cloth. Squeeze it out so it is damp but not dripping. Wrap the cloth around an egg.

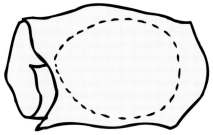

4. Using the eyedropper, add little dabs of color to the cloth. Make designs or pictures. Or just spot the cloth with different colors.

5. When you are done adding color, carefully twist the ends of the cloth to make it tighten around the egg. This will make the colors run into each other.

6. Take the cloth off the egg. Let the egg dry.

 The staff at the Cadbury Red Tulip factory in Ringwood, Victoria, Australia, made a chocolate Easter egg on April 9, 1992, that weighed 10,482 pounds, 14 ounces and was 23 feet, 3 inches high!!! Bet that gave the Easter Bunny a backache!

Egg Scavenger Hunt

Usually kids search for hidden Easter eggs and treats during an egg hunt. But in this more challenging version, everyone gets involved!

You'll need:

pencil

paper

small basket or bag for each family member

colored eggs, candies, flowers, Easter cards, other treats: enough of each treat for the whole family

1. Choose a few places in your house to hide the treats. Try closets, under beds, in cookie jars, or in the bathtub.

2. In each place, hide one type of Easter treat. Be sure there are enough of that treat for your whole family.

3. Think of clues you can give your family to help them find these places. You may need to think of more than one clue for each hiding spot. Write the clues on a piece of paper.

4. To start the hunt, give each family member a basket or bag in which to put his or her treats. Read aloud the first clue for the first hiding spot. Give your family some time to search for the hiding spot. If they have a hard time, read the next clue for that hiding spot.

5. Continue reading clues for the other hiding spots until they find all the treats.

Don't worry if you don't have a lot of treats. If you just hide Easter cards and eggs (which you can make yourself), the hunt will be fun.

Earth Day
April 22

Earth Day began in 1970. This day is set aside each year to remind all of us that we need to take care of the earth.

There are many ways we can help the earth.

We can stop pollution. Trash is polluting lakes, rivers, and oceans. The air is being dirtied by factory smoke and car exhaust. What can you do about this?

We can protect animals. People are hunting animals for their furs and tusks. Some just hunt for fun. Sometimes animals lose their homes because people cut down trees and build parking lots and shopping malls. Many animals are close to being extinct. What can you do about this?

We can reduce trash. We are running out of places to put our trash, and nature is suffering. What can you do about this?

We can save our forests. More and more trees are dying because people use them to make things like furniture and paper. What can you do about this?

Earth Day is a time for you to think about what you can do to help the world around you. It is also a time to tell other people what they can do.

Earth Mobile

Try making small earths in all different sizes and hanging them from the ceiling.

You'll need:

flour

water

tissue paper or newspaper, cut into strips

round balloon

green, brown, and blue
   liquid tempera paints

sewing needle

thread

scissors

atlas or globe

1. Mix together some flour and water until it makes a thin paste.

2. Ask a grown-up to help you blow up the balloon, so it is as big as you want your earth mobile to be.

3. Dip the paper strips in the paste mixture until they are very wet. Place the strips on the balloon until it is completely covered. Be sure to put at least two layers of strips on the balloon. Leave the tied piece of the balloon sticking out.

4. Let the balloon dry for about two days. (STOP) Ask your grown-up helper to cut the tied end of the balloon. The balloon will deflate inside the papier-mâché shell. Pull the balloon out through the hole.

5. Keeping the hole at the top, paint your earth. Use blue to make the water, and brown and green to make land. Look at an atlas or a globe to see where everything goes. When you are done, let it dry completely.

6. (STOP) When the earth has dried, ask your grown-up helper to use the needle to pull a length of thread through the top of the earth. Use the thread to hang your earth mobile.

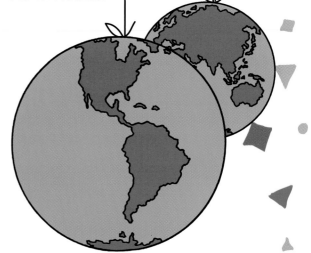

When you recycle something, it is used again, usually to make a new substance. Newspapers, cans, glass, and plastic containers can all be used again instead of just being thrown in a dump. In a year, Americans throw out 50 billion cans, 27 billion glass bottles, and 65 million plastic and metal container covers. If we don't recycle, soon there will be no place to put all that garbage!

Earth Walk

This is a different kind of scavenger hunt, to get you thinking about how you can help the earth.

You'll need:

paper
pencil

Several charity groups in Padua, Italy built a model of a church from 3,245,000 cans. The model was 96 feet by 75 feet by 56 feet. It took 20,000 hours to finish and was completed in 1992. Now they know how to recycle!

1. On a piece of paper, write down some of the problems the earth has, like dirty water, littering, people who cut down trees and don't replace them, people who don't recycle, and other things like that.

2. Find a grown-up to take a walk with you. You can also bring along other friends if you like. Bring your list with you.

3. Walk around your neighborhood, or through a park, or even in your backyard. How many of the problems on your list can you find outside? When you see a problem, put a check next to it. Do you see any other problems that are not on your list? Add them to the list.

4. When you go home, think of ways you can fix some of these problems: start a recycling program, pick up trash in the park, plant some trees, etc. Ask some kid and grown-up friends to help you put your plan into action.

May Day
May 1

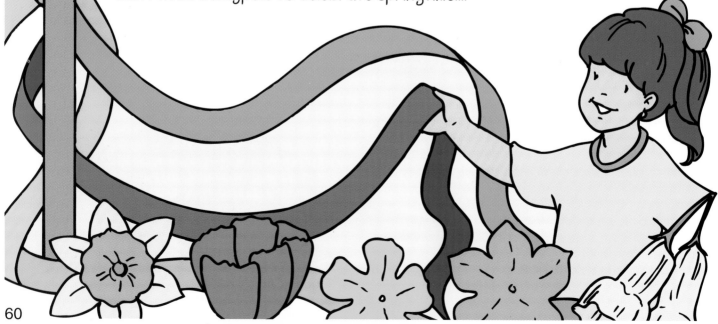

On May Day, people in many countries celebrate springtime. These spring festivals may have started thousands of years ago.

The Romans celebrated the Floralia festival in April. They gathered flowers to honor Flora, the goddess of springtime. Another early people, called the Celts, celebrated a festival called Beltane on May 1. The Celts believed the fairies were very active on Beltane. Eventually, these two holidays were celebrated as one.

Then, in the Middle Ages, the English people began adding their own touches to the festival. They sang songs and gave gifts and danced around a pole with long ribbons attached. As they danced, the people would wrap the ribbons around the maypole so it was colorfully covered when they were done.

In Italy, boys sang to the girls they loved. In Switzerland, boys planted May pine trees under the windows of their sweethearts. In France, Christians believed that the month of May should honor Mary, Jesus's mother. They chose young girls to be the queens of their churches, and held processions to honor Mary and her queens.

May Day is still very popular in England today. But when the English settlers came to America, they did not really celebrate May Day. It has never really become a popular holiday in the United States. But some schools, churches, and groups still have dances and songs, parades, and May queens. But you don't need a maypole to celebrate springtime....

For the Birds

When the birds return to your neighborhood this spring, treat them to a special homecoming meal.

You'll need:

large pinecone
length of string or yarn
1/2 cup vegetable oil
1 cup peanut butter
2 cups birdseed
paper or plastic bag

May Day Folklore

Here are some of the beliefs people once had about May Day:

- It is a day to go barefooted.
- Wash your face with dew before sunrise and your freckles will go away.
- At noon, hold a mirror over a well to see the person you are going to marry.
- If you catch a lot of fish, you will catch fish every day in May.
- You can cure a sore throat by opening your mouth and letting a ray of sunlight shine into it.

1. Tie one end of the string around the bottom of the pinecone.

2. In a small bowl, mix together the oil and peanut butter.

3. Spread the peanut-butter mixture onto the pinecone. Be sure to get some of the mixture in between the petals of the cone.

4. Pour the birdseed into a paper or plastic bag. Place the pinecone in the bag. Carefully shake the bag up and down so the seeds coat the pinecone.

5. 🛑 Ask a grown-up to hang the pinecone from a tree branch.

6. Watch the birds as they stop for a snack.

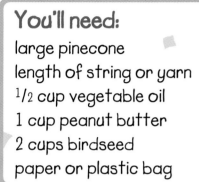

Blooming Garden

Plant flowers on May Day for a beautiful view you'll enjoy for months to come.

You'll need:
small shovel
rake
flower seeds
water

1. Ask a grown-up to help you find a place to put your garden (or use a window box or planter).

2. **STOP** With help, use the shovel to dig up this area. ("Digging up" means to lift and turn over the soil so it is softer and easier to plant the seeds. Also, leave some soil on the side to cover your seeds.)

3. Rake the garden area. Pull out any large rocks or sticks.

4. Plant the seeds according to the directions on the package.

5. Cover the seeds with 1/2 inch of dirt.

6. Spray the garden with water so the soil is moist.

7. Repeat step 6 every day for ten days. Plants should appear in two weeks.

It will take about four to six weeks for your flowers to bloom. If you want flowers to grow again next year, let some of the flowers die off, dry out, and fall to the ground. The seeds will fall into the soil and more flowers should grow next year.

Caterpillar Cake

This fun treat is perfect for a May Day party at school or at home.

You'll need:

angel food cake mix
green food coloring
3 cans white frosting
1 cup coconut
decorations you can
    eat like: M&Ms®, Reese's Pieces®,
    licorice strings, hot cinnamon candies,
    raisins, nuts, chocolate chips, etc.
26 pipe cleaners

1. 🛑 Ask a grown-up to bake the cake in a cupcake tin according to the directions on the box. After mixing and before you bake, add a few drops of food coloring to make the mix green. (Do not use tin liners—spray the cups with cooking spray.)

2. Put a few drops of food coloring in each can of frosting. Mix well until the frosting is completely green.

3. Place the coconut in a plastic bag. Add a few drops of food coloring. Shake the bag until all the coconut is tinted green.

4. When the cupcakes are completely cool, top with the frosting. Decorate the cupcakes with the coconut and candy. Be sure to decorate one cupcake to look like it has eyes.

5. Stick two pipe cleaners (one in each side) in each cupcake. Bend them to look like legs, as shown. Stick two more pipe cleaners in the top of the cupcake with the eyes, to make antennae.

6. To serve, arrange the cupcakes one behind the other on the table. Be sure the one with the eyes is the first cupcake in the line.

7. For more fun, let your guests decorate their own cupcake before you arrange them in a caterpillar shape.

Cinco de Mayo
May 5

Mexicans celebrate May 5 because in 1862 they won an important battle against the French on that date. The French wanted to capture Mexico City and then rule the whole country. In the town of Puebla, the peasants (even women!) fought the French soldiers and won, giving the whole country hope that they could drive the French out of their nation, which they did.

This day is often celebrated with parades. For the parades, people dress up like French and Mexican soldiers. The French soldiers are dressed in traditional uniforms and usually carry bottles of wine. The Mexican peasants are dressed in homemade uniforms, with knives and old-fashioned rifles. Women also march with the soldiers to remember the women who fought at Puebla.

In the afternoon, the "soldiers" act out the Battle of Puebla. Rifles and cannons are fired, and people run around and shout. When it starts to get dark, the two men dressed like the French and Mexican generals act out a sword fight. And the Mexican general always wins.

Sometimes there are speeches during the celebration. The people also enjoy fireworks, barbecues, mariachi bands, and bullfights. And, of course, there is lots of music and delicious food!

Sopaipillas

This traditional Mexican bread can be made without the honey and sugar and served as part of a meal. Or with the sweet glaze, it makes a yummy dessert.

You'll need:

4 cups flour
2 teaspoons baking powder
1 teaspoon salt
4 tablespoons shortening
1 1/2 cups warm water
shortening
honey or cinnamon-sugar mixture
powdered sugar

1. Combine the flour, baking powder, and salt in a bowl. **STOP** Ask a grown-up to cut in the shortening.

2. Make a well in the center of the ingredients by digging out the middle. Pour the water into the hole. With your hands, mix the water and the dry mixture together. Knead the dough until it is smooth. Cover the bowl with a towel and let it sit for 20 minutes.

3. **STOP** Ask your helper to heat a 2-inch square of shortening in a heavy pan on medium heat.

4. Spread a little flour on a cutting board. Roll out the dough until it is about 1/8 inch thick.

5. **STOP** Ask your grown-up helper to cut the dough into 4-inch squares. Fry the squares in the pan, turning once, until they are golden on both sides. (The sopaipillas will puff and become hollow when they are heated.)

6. **STOP** Ask a grown-up to drain the sopaipillas on paper towels.

7. Glaze the sopaipillas with honey or cinnamon-sugar. Sprinkle the powdered sugar on top.

Fun Fact:
The capital of Mexico is Mexico City. About 12 million people live in the capital. If all those people joined hands, the line they made would stretch halfway around the world!

66

Making Maracas

Music is a special part of a Cinco de Mayo celebration.
Make these easy rhythm instruments to give away
as favors or to play with the band.

You'll need:

unpopped popcorn kernels
2 deflated balloons
tape
2 toilet tissue tubes
1 box Knox® gelatin
1/3 cup plus 2 teaspoons white glue
1/4 cup water
newspaper cut in strips
pin
paints
paintbrush
glitter
glue

1. Place some popcorn kernels inside one balloon. With help, blow up the balloon. Tie the end closed. Repeat with the second balloon.

2. Tape each balloon to one of the toilet tissue tubes.

3. Mix together the gelatin, glue, and water. Stir until it is smooth. You've made papier-mâché mix.

4. Dip a newspaper strip into the mixture until it is completely wet. Place the strip on one of the balloons. Continue dipping strips and placing them on the balloon. Keep doing this until the balloon and tube are completely covered. Repeat this with the second balloon. Let the papier-mâché dry overnight.

5. When the papier-mâché is completely dry, push a pin into the top of each maraca, where the balloon is. When you shake your maracas now, you will hear the popcorn kernels rattling around.

6. Decorate the maracas with paint and glitter. Now you're ready to play along with the band!

Mother's Day
Second Sunday in May

On Mother's Day, people tell their mothers how special they are. They make and send her cards. Some children serve their mother breakfast in bed, and spend the whole day doing things for her, so she doesn't have to do any work. Florists are very busy on this day, because people like to send their mothers flowers. People sometimes wear colorful carnations if their mother is still alive, and white carnations if she isn't. It is a way to honor your mother.

Mother's Day became an official holiday in 1915, the year after President Woodrow Wilson recommended to Congress that mothers should have their own special day of honor. But people had been hoping for a mother's day for years and years before that.

In 1872, a woman named Julia Ward Howe suggested that the United States should celebrate a Mother's Day holiday. Once a year, she would hold a Mother's Day meeting in Boston. In 1887, a schoolteacher in Kentucky, Mary Towles Sasseen, started running yearly celebrations. By 1904, a man named Frank E. Hering decided to campaign to get the day officially recognized.

In 1907, Anna Jarvis of West Virginia chose the second Sunday of May and urged people to honor their mothers on that day. She began the custom of wearing a carnation on Mother's Day. In 1908, churches began to hold Mother's Day celebrations. Finally, the General Conference of the Methodist Episcopal Church named Anna Jarvis the founder of Mother's Day. Shortly after this, President Wilson suggested a national celebration.

Easy French Toast

*French toast is usually fried in a pan,
but with this easy baked recipe,
you can whip up breakfast for Mom in no time.*

You'll need:

1/4 cup margarine, melted
1/2 cup brown sugar
1/2 teaspoon cinnamon
2 eggs
1/4 cup milk
1/2 teaspoon vanilla or
    almond extract
6 slices of Italian bread

1. (STOP) Ask a grown-up to heat the oven to
375°.

2. Pour the margarine into a baking pan.

3. Combine the brown sugar and
cinnamon. Sprinkle this mixture into the
baking pan.

4. Mix the eggs and milk together.
Stir well. Add the vanilla or
almond extract.

5. Dip each piece of bread in the egg
mixture. Coat both sides. Lay the bread
slices in the baking pan. When all the
bread slices are in the pan, pour the rest
of the egg mixture over them.

6. Cover the pan with aluminum foil. (STOP) Bake
the French toast for about 25 minutes
with the cover on. Then take the foil off
and bake for another 10 minutes.

To serve the French toast, put one or
two slices on each plate. You can top
each plate with berries, syrup, jam,
whipped cream, banana slices, or
whatever else you like.

In the 1700s, a woman in
Russia gave birth to 69
children. She was mother to 16
pairs of twins, seven sets of triplets, and
four sets of quadruplets. Now, that's a
Supermom!

Gift Soaps

Mom can use these pretty homemade soap balls for a luxurious bath or to make closets and drawers smell sweet.

Makes five 2-inch balls

You'll need:

2 cups Ivory® Soap Flakes
1/4 cup water
food coloring
fragrance or flavor extract

1. Mix the water, food coloring, and extract together. Use as much coloring and extract as you need to get the smell and color you want.

2. Add the soap flakes and mix until it is crumbly.

3. Shape the mixture into five balls. Make sure each ball is packed together tightly. Be sure to pat and shape the balls so they are smooth.

To wrap the soap balls, wrap each one in a square of netting and tie with a ribbon. You can put them in a small basket or a pretty bowl to present them to Mom. These are also nice gifts for aunts and grandmas.

Carnation Bouquet

*Carnations are the traditional
flowers of Mother's Day.*

You'll need:

different colors of crepe paper
   (including green)
floral wire, cut into
   8-inch "stems"
floral tape
scissors
ribbon
perfume
tracing paper

1. Trace the leaf shape below. (STOP) With help, cut out the leaf shape.

2. Trace the leaf shape onto the green paper, six to eight times for each flower you make. (STOP) With help, cut out the leaf shapes.

3. (STOP) For each flower, cut a 3-inch piece of crepe paper. Cut fringes on the edge of the paper strip, as shown below.

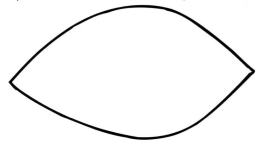

4. Gather the unfringed side of the paper, as shown below. Wrap one end of a length of floral wire around the uncut side.

5. Wrap the floral tape around the wire to cover the stem. Place four to five paper leaves at the top of the wire and wrap the tape around them to keep them in place, as shown. As you wrap your way down the stem, place a paper leaf here and there.

6. When the flowers are finished, spray them with perfume. Tie them all to-gether into a bouquet with a piece of ribbon.

Memorial Day
Last Monday in May

On Memorial Day, we honor the men and women who died fighting for this country.

Memorial Day began in 1866 in Waterloo, New York. The people there closed their shops. They flew their flags at half-mast. They put flowers and other decorations on the graves of soldiers who died in the Civil War. People have been honoring fallen soldiers from all our wars ever since.

On Memorial Day, there are often parades and ceremonies. People put flags and flowers on soldiers' graves. Sometimes there are speeches. Often these speeches will include lines from Abraham Lincoln's famous speech, the Gettysburg Address. Lincoln gave that speech to dedicate a cemetery for fallen Civil War soldiers.

This day has also been called Poppy Day since the end of World War I. You may see people on the street selling little paper poppies. The money that they make is donated to help men who were hurt while fighting in a war.

Here are a few lines from The Gettysburg Address. What do you think President Lincoln was saying?

Four score and seven years ago our fathers brought forth upon this continent a new nation, conceived in Liberty, and dedicated to the proposition that all men are created equal....we are highly resolved that the dead shall not have died in vain—that the nation shall, under God, have a new birth of freedom—and that governments of the people, by the people, and for the people, shall not perish from the earth.

Memorial Day Poppies

Red poppies have become the symbol of memory and support for American soldiers. Veterans groups sell poppies to raise money for disabled veterans.

You'll need:

red crepe paper
pencil
scissors
green pipe cleaners
safety pins
ruler

1. Draw a 4-inch circle on a piece of crepe paper. (STOP) Ask a grown-up to help you cut the circle out.

2. Trace around the circle to make another circle outline on the crepe paper. (STOP) Cut out the second circle.

3. Place one circle on top of the other. (STOP) Ask a grown-up to help you poke two holes in the middle of the circles.

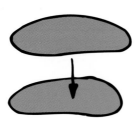

4. Weave the pipe cleaner through the holes, as shown below. Wrap the short end of the pipe cleaner around the long end to fasten it and make a stem.

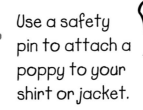

5. Use a safety pin to attach a poppy to your shirt or jacket.

Fun Fact:

Many foods that you eat every day were originally created for our soldiers. These include granola bars, instant noodle soup, freeze-dried coffee, and M&Ms®. One treat we haven't seen in stores is Hershey's Desert Bar. Created for soldiers fighting in the Gulf War, the chocolate bar can withstand temperatures up to 140° without melting.

Patriot Cake

Here's a yummy dessert that celebrates the red, white, and blue.

You'll need:

package of white cake mix
red and blue food coloring
whipped topping
red and blue sugar crystals or
sprinkles

1. Prepare the cake mix according to directions on the box. Pour the batter into a 9-inch by 12-inch cake pan.

2. Squeeze a few drops of the red and blue food coloring on top of the batter. Swirl a fork through the batter.

3. STOP Bake and cool the cake according to the box directions.

4. When the cake is completely cooled, spread the whipped topping on top. Sprinkle on the sugar crystals or sprinkles. When you cut and serve the cake, each piece will have red and blue swirls!

You can use fresh blueberries, strawberries, and raspberries to top this cake instead of sugar crystals. You can try making a flag design with the berries!

Father's Day
Third Sunday in June

Happy Father's Day, Dad!

On Father's Day we show our fathers how much we love them. We make them special cards. Sometimes we buy them gifts like ties or golf clubs. Mom might bake a cake or make a special dinner.

Father's Day only became an official holiday in 1972, when President Richard M. Nixon signed Father's Day into law. But people had been trying to make the holiday official since 1909.

A woman named Sonora Louise Smart Dodd from Spokane, Washington, was listening to a sermon in church on Mother's Day in 1909. It made her think that there should be a special day to honor fathers. When she was a little girl, her mother died. Her father raised six children all by himself.

Sonora worked hard to make sure Father's Day was celebrated, and in 1910 Spokane honored fathers for the first time. From that time on, people continued to work to make it an official holiday for the whole country.

Blueberry Muffins For Dad

*Bake a batch of these yummy muffins
and serve Dad breakfast in bed.*

Makes about a dozen

You'll need:

1 egg, beaten
1/2 cup milk
1/4 cup oil
1 1/2 cups flour
1 cup sugar
2 teaspoons baking powder
1/2 teaspoon salt
1 cup blueberries
1/3 cup flour
1/2 teaspoon cinnamon
1/4 cup margarine, softened

1. STOP Ask a grown-up to preheat the oven to 400°.

2. Put one paper liner in each cup of a muffin tin.

3. Stir together the egg, milk, and oil.

4. Add the flour, 1/2 cup of the sugar, the baking powder, and the salt. Mix well. Fold in the blueberries.

5. In a separate bowl, use your hands to combine the rest of the sugar with the flour, cinnamon, and margarine. Mix until it makes little crumbs.

6. Pour the batter into the muffin cups until they are 2/3 full.

7. Sprinkle a tablespoon of the crumbly mixture on top of the batter in each muffin cup.

8. STOP Bake the muffins for 20 minutes, until they are golden brown.

Dad's Miniature Golf Course

If your dad likes golf, challenge him to a game in the backyard for Father's Day.

You'll need:

9 different-sized cans (be sure they are big enough for a golf ball to fit inside)

scissors

golf clubs or broomsticks or yardsticks with small sponges tied to the end

golf balls

objects to use as course challenges: chairs, boxes, toys, houseplants, hats, teddy bears, etc.

paper

pen

1. To set up the course, scatter the cans around the backyard. Lay them on their sides so the golf balls can roll inside.

2. Once you have the nine holes set up, set up obstacles. Put chairs over the holes, put plants in front of the hole, or scatter toys around the hole. Make the first few holes easy, and make the last holes hard.

3. To play the game, each player needs a club and a golf ball. Taking turns, each player stands the same distance from the hole and tries to hit a golf ball so it goes into the can.

4. To keep score, count the number of times each player must hit the ball before it goes into the hole. Write that number down. Add up all the numbers for each player at the end of the game. The player with the lowest score wins.

Memo Holder

Dad can use this handy gift at home or at the office.

You'll need:

waxed paper
supply of Popsicle® sticks
glue
paint
paintbrush
glitter
construction paper
scissors
paper cut into 3-inch by 4-inch squares

1. Place a piece of waxed paper on the table. Lay 11 Popsicle® sticks side by side on the waxed paper as shown. Be sure the sticks are very close together.

2. Run a thick line of glue down both sides of the Popsicle® stick row as shown . Let the glue dry.

3. Lay seven Popsicle® sticks on the waxed paper side by side. Run a thick line of glue down both sides of the sticks. Repeat this step with two more sticks. Let the glue dry.

4. Lay one Popsicle® stick on the waxed paper. Run a thin line of glue over the stick as shown below. Stack another stick on top. Do this until you have a stack of eight sticks, one on top of the other. Let the stack dry.

5. Repeat step 4 to make a second stack of sticks.

6. When each part is dry, glue the memo holder together. Glue each stick stack to one side of the 11-stick back as shown below. Glue the seven-stick piece on top. Let it dry.

7. Glue the end of one stick to the end of another to form a right angle as shown. Glue the free ends of each stick to the back of the memo holder to make a hanger.

8. Use paints, glitter, and construction paper to decorate the memo holder any way you like. Put the paper squares inside the memo holder before you give it to Dad.

Summer
End of June Through Middle of September

Don't you just love summer? Summer means no school. It means staying up later. It means swimming in a pool, an ocean, or a lake. It means car trips and plane trips and all kinds of fun vacations.

Summer is the warmest season of the year. In countries on the top half of the earth, it is summer from June through September. In countries on the bottom half of the earth, summer is from December through March.

In the summer, you probably like to do things that keep you cool. You probably like to play outside a lot. Summer is the perfect time to make up your own games. It is the perfect time to try something new.

Travel Tic-Tac-Toe

Here is a great game for beating boredom on long car trips.

You'll need:

9-inch loop side strip of Velcro®,
  cut into nine equal pieces
12-inch hook side strip of Velcro®,
  cut into 10 equal pieces
10-inch square piece of felt
five 10-inch lengths of ribbon
glue
two 8½-inch by 11-inch pieces of
  tagboard, each a different color
2½ inch cardboard circle
one small plastic bag
scissors
marker

1. Glue four ribbons onto the felt square to make a tic-tac-toe board, as shown.

2. Glue a piece of loop-side Velcro® in the center of each tic-tac-toe square.

3. Use the cardboard circle to trace six circles onto each piece of tagboard. (STOP) Cut out the circles with help.

4. On the back of each circle, glue one piece of hook-side Velcro®. You can decorate the front of each circle any way you like, but be sure you can still see the background color.

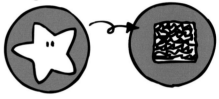

5. Place one dot of glue in the center of the back of the felt square. Fold the fifth ribbon in half to find the middle of the ribbon. Press the center of the ribbon onto the glue dot. Let it dry.

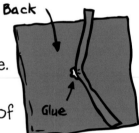

6. To play, each player gets six circles, all the same color. Take turns placing circles in the tic-tac-toe squares until one of you gets three in a row in any direction.

7. When you are done playing, place all the playing pieces in the plastic bag. Tie the bag closed with the ribbon on the back of the felt square.

The Name Game

Robert

Marcus!

You can play this fun game anytime, anywhere.

Tasha!

For at least 2 players

You'll need:

paper
pencil

1. On the paper, list the names of all the players.

2. The first player says a name out loud.

3. The next player says a name that begins with the last letter from the name that the first player said.

4. Players take turns thinking of names that begin with the last letter in the name said by the player who went before.

5. If a player can't think of a name, he is stumped. When a player gets stumped, you write the letter "N" next to his name. If he gets stumped again, you write the letter "A." Every time a player is stumped, you write the next letter of the word "NAME" beside his name on the paper. When a player gets stumped four times and spells out the word "NAME," he is out of the game. The last player left in the game is the winner.

6. When a player is stumped, the next player continues the game. She must think of a name that begins with the letter that stumped the last player. If no player can think of a name for that letter, the game is over.

Stacy !

Adam!

Patty N
Mike   NAM
Gina   N

Do you like traveling by car? The longest highway in the world, the Pan-American Highway, stretches from northwest Alaska down to Chile and then over to Brasilia, Brazil. Now that's a road trip!

S'mores

These yummy treats are traditional camping-trip snacks.

Be sure an adult is there to help you at all times when you are near the campfire.

You'll need:
marshmallows
chocolate bars
graham crackers
long sticks
campfire

1. Place a piece of chocolate on top of a graham cracker.

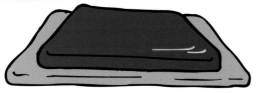

2. STOP Ask a grown-up to help you toast two marshmallows over the campfire.

3. Place the two marshmallows on top of the piece of chocolate. Cover the marshmallows with another graham cracker.

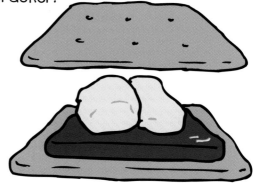

4. Gently press down on the s'more to keep it closed. When the chocolate starts to melt, it's ready to eat!

Canada Day
July 1

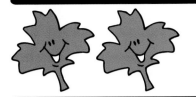
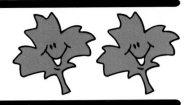

The people of Canada celebrate their Independence Day on Canada Day. The celebration is a lot like July 4th festivities in the United States. It is one of Canada's most important national holidays.

On July 1, 1867, the British colonies of New Brunswick, Nova Scotia, and the Province of Canada joined together as one country. The new nation's name was the Dominion of Canada. (Canada Day was called Dominion Day until 1982.) Until that day, they had been completely ruled by the British.

When the colonies joined together, they created a House of Commons and a Senate to govern the land. Britain still handled their foreign affairs. That means the British government was in charge when Canada had to deal with other countries. In 1931, Canada took over its own foreign affairs when British Parliament passed an act declaring the nation independent. Canada still has very strong ties with Great Britain. Many Canadians still recognize the Queen of England as their own queen.

Just like the Fourth of July festivities in the United States, Canada Day is celebrated with picnics, parades, and fireworks. A special week-long festival is held in the bordering cities of Windsor, Ontario, and Detroit, Michigan, to recognize the two Independence Days. The celebration is called the International Freedom Festival. It includes concerts and art exhibits, as well as fireworks and water parades.

Maple Leaf Sugar Cookies

These delicious cookies will put everyone in the patriotic mood.

Makes 2 dozen big cookies

You'll need:

$3/4$ cup margarine
1 cup sugar
2 eggs
$1/2$ teaspoon vanilla
$2 1/2$ cups flour
1 teaspoon baking powder
1 teaspoon salt
1 can vanilla frosting
red sugar crystals
maple extract
maple leaf-shaped cookie cutter (if you don't have one, any kind of cookie cutter will do)

1. Mix together the margarine, sugar, eggs, and vanilla. Blend well.

2. Add flour, baking powder, and salt to the mixture. Mix until well blended.

3. Place the dough in the refrigerator for one hour.

4. Sprinkle a cutting board with flour. With help, use a rolling pin to roll the dough out on the board until it is $1/8$ inch thick.

5. Cut out the dough with the cookie cutter. Place the leaf-shaped cookies on an ungreased cookie sheet.

6. STOP Bake the cookies in a 400° oven for six to eight minutes. They should be lightly browned when you take them out of the oven. Let the cookies cool.

7. Add a few drops of maple extract to the vanilla frosting. Mix thoroughly. Spread the frosting on the cookies when they have cooled. Sprinkle on the sugar crystals.

Fun Fact:
Maple leaves are the national symbol of Canada. In the summer, the leaves of the maple tree are green. But in the fall, they turn bright red.

Firecracker Dessert

Canada Day is often celebrated with fireworks displays. Light up the night with this delicious treat!

Serves 8

You'll need:

1/2 gallon vanilla ice cream or
  frozen yogurt
1 1/2 cups sliced strawberries
1 1/2 cups raspberries
strawberry syrup
whipped topping
sugar cubes
lemon extract
eyedropper

This dessert must be served immediately after it's made.

1. Place the raspberries in the bottom of a medium-sized glass mixing bowl.

2. Spoon half the vanilla ice cream on top of the raspberries. The ice cream does not need to completely cover the raspberries.

3. Place the strawberries on top of the ice cream.

4. Spoon the rest of the vanilla ice cream on top of the strawberries.

5. Pour the strawberry syrup over the vanilla ice cream.

6. Spread the whipped topping over the dessert until the top is completely covered.

7. Place the sugar cubes on the whipped topping. Use the eyedropper to place a little lemon extract on each cube.

8. Place the dessert dish on the table where it will be served. **STOP** Ask a grown-up to use a match to light each sugar cube. Let the flames burn. When they stop burning, remove the sugar cubes. Spoon the dessert into dessert dishes.

Independence Day
July 4

America was once ruled by the British. But the people who lived here, the colonists, were not very happy with all the laws. They wanted to make their own rules. They decided to declare this a new nation.

The group of men who did this, the Continental Congress, made the decision on July 2, 1776. They prepared a written announcement. That announcement was called the Declaration of Independence. They signed it on July 4, 1776.

This date is celebrated every year on the Fourth of July, or Independence Day. People call it the birthday of the United States.

The Declaration of Independence lists all the reasons that the colonists did not want the British to rule them anymore. It was written by Thomas Jefferson, with help from Benjamin Franklin and John Adams. The declaration says two things that are very important. First, it says that people who rule a country should serve the people of that country. Second, it says that all people are created equal. These two ideas are thought to be right and truthful even today.

The men of the Continental Congress were very happy about declaring the country free. John Adams said that the day would be celebrated by all Americans in the future as a great festival. He said it should include "pomp and parade, with shows, games, sports, guns, bells, bonfires, and illuminations, from one end of this continent to the other, from this time forward for evermore." Our Independence Day festivities today include many of these things. One of our favorite ways to celebrate this holiday is with fancy fireworks displays.

The Declaration of Independence was printed on a piece of parchment. All the members of the Continental Congress signed it. You can see that piece of parchment at the National Archives Building in Washington, DC.

Hot Dog Roll-Ups

*Serve this dressed-up version of
hot dogs at your July 4th barbecue.*

You'll need:

hot dogs
refrigerated crescent rolls
1 onion, cut into thick slices
slices of cheddar or
   American cheese

1. (STOP) Cut a slice down the length of each hot dog.

2. Spray a skillet with nonstick cooking spray. (STOP) Ask a grown-up to brown the hot dogs and onion in the skillet for about two minutes. Remove the hot dogs from the pan.

3. Let the onions cook until they are browned.

4. Place some onions into the slit in each hot dog.

5. Place one slice of cheese on top of the onions.

6. Unroll the crescent rolls. Lay one hot dog on each roll. Roll the crescents around the hot dogs. Lay the hot dogs on a baking sheet.

7. (STOP) Bake the hot dogs in a 350° oven until the cheese melts and the crescent rolls are golden brown (about ten minutes).

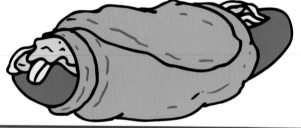

In the 1800s, rodeos were a popular way of celebrating Independence Day. In 1882, ranchmen in Nebraska held an "Old Glory Blowout." About a thousand cowboys were involved in activities like horse races, shooting contests, driving buffalo, and plays that included attacking a stagecoach.

The man who organized it was named William Cody. The rodeo show went over so well that Cody took it all over the country. He became known as Buffalo Bill, and the rodeo became Buffalo Bill's Wild West Show. The show traveled the world for more than 30 years.

88

Freedom Flag

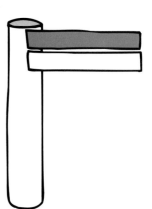

Decorate your backyard for that holiday barbecue with these special flags.

You'll need:

paper towel tube (one for each flag decoration)

9-inch by 12-inch sheets of red and white construction paper

scissors

glue

ruler

4 1/2-inch by 6-inch square of blue construction paper (one for each flag)

silver glitter

1. Wrap white construction paper around the paper towel tube. (STOP) Ask a grown-up to help you cut off the extra paper. Glue the ends of the paper together so the paper is tightly wrapped around the roll.

2. (STOP) Ask a grown-up to cut four 1-inch by 12-inch strips from red construction paper and three 1-inch by 12-inch strips from the white construction paper.

3. Glue one end of one red strip to the tube as shown. Underneath the red strip, glue the end of a white strip as shown. Glue on another red strip, then a white strip, a red strip, then a white strip, and one last red strip. You should have seven strips in all.

4. Glue the blue rectangle on top of the first four strips as shown.

5. Place dots of glue on the blue rectangle and sprinkle on the glitter. When dry, shake off the extra glitter.

Fun Fact:

The United States flag has 13 stripes, one for each of the original 13 colonies. There are 50 stars, one for each state in the union. The last star was added in 1960, when Hawaii became a state.

Paper Poppers

Make this safe version of a firecracker.

You'll need:

two 8-inch squares of construction paper
glue
8-inch square of typewriter
   or printer paper
scissors
tape
confetti

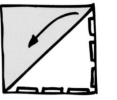

1. Glue the two construction-paper squares together.

2. Fold the printer-paper square in half diagonally. Unfold the square. **STOP** Cut the square in half along the fold. Now you have two triangles.

3. Lay one of the triangles on top of the construction-paper square, as shown below. Tape the triangle to the square on the sides.

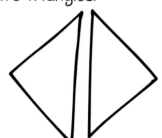

4. Fold the square in half diagonally, making a fold in the white triangle shape, as shown.

5. Place some confetti inside the pocket made by the white triangle.

6. To pop your popper, hold on to the corner that is opposite the white triangle. The fold should face the ceiling. Snap your wrist downward. The triangle will pop out and make a noise.

Bastille Day
July 14

Bastille Day is a favorite national holiday in France. It is like our Independence Day celebration. On July 14, 1789, the people of France stormed the Bastille and captured it.

The Bastille was a prison. To the people of France, it was a symbol of how unfairly the king of France treated them. The king only cared about helping the rich get richer. People with a lot of money did not have to pay taxes, but the poor people were taxed heavily. If the people complained, they were thrown in the Bastille.

The people who attacked the Bastille thought they would find guns and other weapons inside. They wanted to use them to attack the king and his army. The crowd that captured the prison began to tear it down.

The attack of the Bastille was the beginning of the French Revolution. The French king and queen, Louis XVI and Marie Antoinette, were put to death. Kings would never again be the sole rulers of France. Eventually, Napoleon Bonaparte, a French general , took over the government. The French celebrate this day as the beginning of a new freedom for the people of their nation.

The people of France celebrate this national holiday with parades, music, dances, parties, and fireworks. The only time there were no Bastille Day celebrations was during World War II.

Crêpes

This is a popular food in France, and can be filled with almost anything.

Makes 4 servings

You'll need:

1 1/2 cups flour
1 tablespoon sugar
2 cups milk
2 eggs
1 teaspoon vanilla
2 tablespoons margarine, melted
cooking spray
1 cup fresh fruit, sliced
whipped topping

1. Combine the flour, sugar, milk, eggs, vanilla, and margarine. STOP Ask a grown-up to beat the mixture with an electric mixer until it is smooth.

2. Chill in the refrigerator for 30 minutes.

3. Spray a skillet with the cooking spray. STOP Ask a grown-up to heat the pan on medium. Pour enough batter into the pan to cover the bottom. (This should be a thin coat of batter, so spread it with the back of a spoon if it does not cover easily.)

Cook the crêpe until it is lightly browned. Flip it over and cook until the other side is lightly browned.

4. Place the crêpe on a serving plate. Spoon the fruit into the center of the crêpe. Fold over both sides. Serve with whipped cream on top.

5. Repeat steps 3 and 4 until you've used all the batter.

A super-size crêpe was made and flipped in England in 1994. The crêpe weighed 6,614 pounds and measured more than 49 feet around!

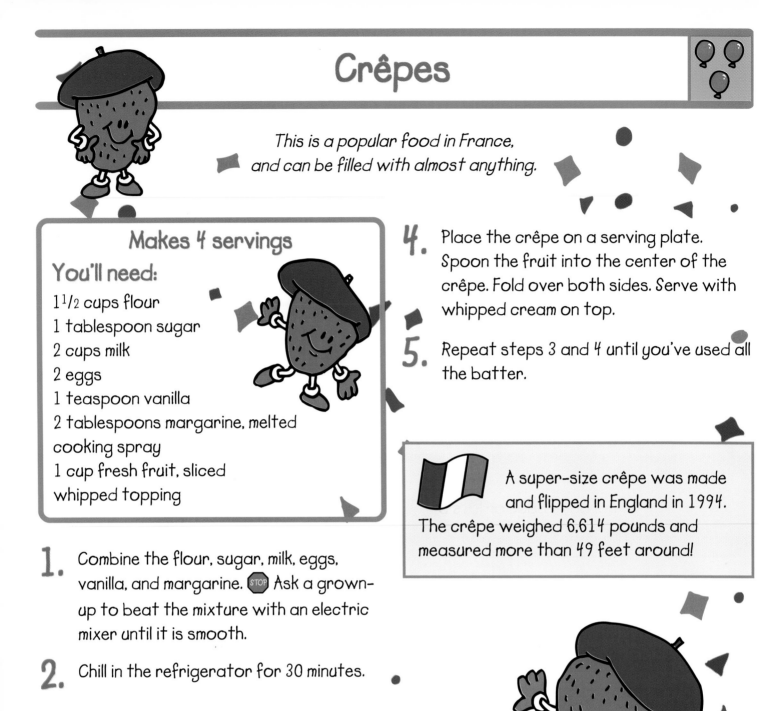

92

Fireworks T-Shirt

The French people celebrate Bastille Day with fireworks displays. The design on this snazzy T-shirt looks like beautiful fireworks popping and exploding!

You'll need:

white T-shirt

flat gift box

squirt gun and/or plastic spray bottles (one for each color of paint)

several colors of fabric dye or fabric paint (if paint is used, make a mixture that is one part paint and three parts water)

glitter

fabric glue

several plastic garbage bags or lots of old newspapers

old clothes or an artist's smock

Do this project outside or cover the floor inside with the bags or newspapers! And don't forget to wear old clothes. It gets pretty messy!

1. Stretch the shirt over the gift box.

2. Fill the squirt gun or spray bottles with the dye or paint mixture.

3. If you are outside, lean the gift box and shirt against a tree so it is standing up and facing you. If you are inside, lean it against a wall, but be sure to tape plastic bags or newspaper onto the wall first.

4. Squirt the guns or bottles at the shirt to make fireworks designs. Try your best to keep the paint on the shirt, so you don't make too much of a mess!

5. Let the shirt dry completely. Use the glue to add glitter to the design. Let the shirt dry completely before you wear it.

Labor Day
First Monday in September

Labor Day is a special day honoring working people. Schools and offices are closed. People rest and relax. Sometimes, there are special festivities planned by groups that support and help working people, such as labor unions. But usually it is a day that people spend with their friends and families.

The first Labor Day parade was held in New York City in September 1882. It was organized by two men, Matthew Maguire and Peter J. McGuire. They were the first to suggest that there should be a national holiday to honor working people. The first official Labor Day was in Oregon in 1887. And in 1894, President Grover Cleveland made Labor Day a national holiday.

Many people also think of Labor Day as the official end of summer. Schools usually open around Labor Day. Many beaches and parks close for the season. Everyone knows that cooler weather is just around the corner. Many people go on their last trip to the beach or hold their last big summer cookout on this day.

Twenty Job Questions

Here is a fun game to play with your family while relaxing on Labor Day. Or let Mom and Dad sleep late and play quietly with your brother or sister.

You'll need:
paper (optional)
pencils (optional)

1. One player thinks of a job. Don't tell the other players.

2. The other players take turns asking "yes or no" questions about that job. Players can take notes with the paper and pencils.

3. Try to guess what the job is by the way the player answers the questions.

4. The first player to guess the job correctly is the winner, and thinks of the next job for everyone to guess.

Good questions to ask: Do they wear a uniform? Do they wear a suit? Do they work outside? Do they help people? Do they work in a hospital?

Do they wear uniforms?

No.

A man in Japan began working at a sugar mill in 1872. He retired in 1970 at the age of 105 after working for 98 years!

Grandparents Day
First Sunday after Labor Day

On Grandparents Day, we show Grandma and Grandpa that we love them and care about them. This holiday began in 1978.

This is a great day for making special cards for Grandma and Grandpa. Or you can draw them a picture, give them flowers, or make them a little gift. But the most important thing you can do on Grandparents Day is to spend time with them, and enjoy their company.

And remember, you can honor other people besides your real grandparents on this day. Older relatives and friends of the family will also enjoy celebrating your love and respect.

Wonderful Memory Boxes

*You can keep the good times you share with
your grandparents forever in this special box.*

4. Decorate the construction-paper strip with things that remind you of your grandparents. You can draw and paint pictures, glue in photographs, or attach tickets and flyers from movies you've seen together.

5. As you make more memories with your grandparents, add more pages to the box.

You'll need:

shirt box (at least 8 1/2 inches by 11 inches)
construction paper
glue
tape
paints, markers, crayons

1. Lay a few sheets of paper side by side on a table so that the long edges are touching. Tape the edges together.

2. Place the bottom of the shirt box on the table. Glue the first sheet in your paper "row" to the inside of the box, so it lies flat. The rest of the paper row should fold neatly into the box.

3. Use the paints, markers, and crayons to decorate the outside of the memory box.

Idea: If you don't live near your grandparents, you can make a memory box for them! Attach pictures of yourself, drawings and stories you did in school, and other items to show them what you have been doing since you last saw them. Mail the box to your grandparents, or give it to them the next time you see them.

Family Tree

Grandparents are great people to ask about your family history.

You'll need:

a large piece of tagboard
a pencil

1. Draw a family tree outline like the one on the next page.

2. Ask your grandparents and other family members to help you fill in the tree. As you learn more about your family tree, you can add "branches" and make your tree bigger than the one shown here.

Notes about family trees:

- A straight line between two people that are next to each other means they are married.

  | mom | — | dad |

- If you have a stepmom or stepdad, and you want them added to the tree also, you can do this:

  | mom | — | dad | — | stepmom |
  | me | | step-brother |

- Brothers and sisters are placed next to each other, without any lines connecting them.

  | brother | you | sister |

- Children are listed underneath their parents; a line is drawn from the child's name to the line that connects the two parents' names.

  | mom | dad |
  | brother | you | sister |

- Write each person's full name. You may also want to put his or her birthdate.

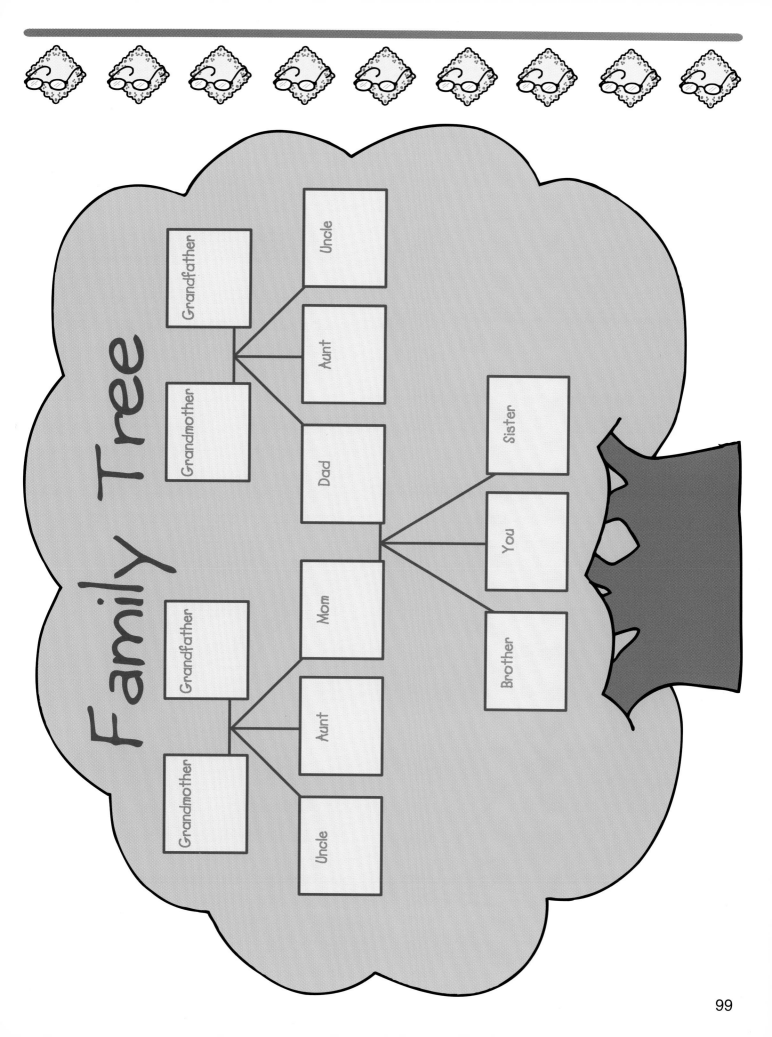

Family Tree

Interview Your Grandparents

Get the "scoop" on your family when you interview your grandparents. This is a great way to spend time with them on Grandparents Day, or any other day.

You'll need:

pencil
paper

1. Set up a time to interview one or both of your grandparents.

2. Make a list of questions you would like to ask. You can ask questions about your grandparent's life, about other members of your family, or anything else.

3. Take notes during the interview, or record it with a tape recorder.

4. When the interview is over, you can write a story about your grandparents in your journal or for your family newsletter.

Note: It is also fun to tape-record or videotape the interview and save it as a nice memory for you and your grandparents.

Rosh Hashanah
Two Days in September or October

Rosh Hashanah is the Jewish New Year. It is one of the holiest days on the Jewish calendar.

Rosh Hashanah is a time when Jews look back at what they have done with the past year, and decide what they will do in the year to come. They ask for forgiveness. It is such an important holiday that it is called a High Holy Day.

At the synagogue services on Rosh Hashanah, a ram's horn, called a *shofar*, is blown. The high-pitched sound of the horn reminds Jewish families to think about their lives and decide what they need to change.

Rosh Hashanah is the beginning of a ten day period known as the Days of Awe. Jews plan for what they will change in the coming year. At the end of these ten days is another High Holy Day, Yom Kippur.

Yom Kippur means Day of Cleansing. On that day, Jews do not go to school or to work, and they do not eat until sundown. *Fasting*, or NOT eating, reminds Jews they need God and other people if they want to eat.

On Yom Kippur many Jews wear white to the synagogue. It symbolizes freshness. After many days of putting the past year behind, Yom Kippur is a celebration of beginning again.

Honey Cake

Jewish families serve nothing bitter or sour on this holiday.
This sweet cake is another way of wishing good luck for the new year.

You'll need:

4 eggs
1 cup sugar
1 cup honey
3/4 cup coffee
1/2 cup melted margarine
4 cups sifted unbleached white flour
3 teaspoons baking powder
1 1/2 teaspoons baking soda
1/4 teaspoon ground cloves
1/4 teaspoon ground nutmeg
1/4 teaspoon ground cinnamon
1/4 cup chopped walnuts
1/4 cup seedless raisins
1/2 teaspoon almond extract
whipped cream

1. (STOP) Ask a grown-up to preheat the oven to 350°. Grease a 14-inch by 10-inch baking pan.

2. (STOP) Use an electric mixer to beat the eggs and sugar in a large bowl until the mixture is fluffy.

3. In a small bowl, stir together the honey and coffee.

4. Stir the melted margarine into the egg and sugar mixture. Then add the honey and coffee mixture to the large bowl.

5. In another bowl, mix together the flour, baking powder, baking soda, and spices. Add the nuts and raisins.

6. Add the flour mixture to the wet mixture. STOP Use an electric mixer to beat the ingredients until they are blended and smooth.

7. Stir in the almond extract.

8. Pour the batter into the pan. STOP Bake the cake for one hour.

9. To serve, cut the cake in squares and top with whipped cream. You can sprinkle cinnamon and sugar on top of the cream, if you like.

Hallah Bread

This bread is often shaped like a ladder to help the family's prayers reach heaven.

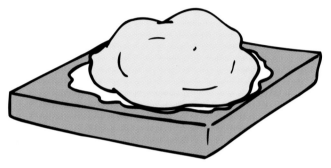

You'll need:

1 package dry yeast
1 cup warm water
1 teaspoon salt
2 tablespoons sugar
3 eggs
2 teaspoons vegetable oil
3 1/2 cups unbleached white flour
1/4 cup poppy seeds (optional)

1. Pour the yeast into a large bowl. Add the water and mix until the yeast dissolves. Stir in the salt and sugar until they dissolve.

2. STOP Use an electric mixer to beat in two eggs and the oil. Slowly stir in three cups of flour.

3. Sprinkle the rest of the flour onto a large cutting board. Place the dough on the board. Knead the dough with your hands for a few minutes.

4. Put the dough back in the bowl. Cover it with a cloth or towel that you have run under the faucet and wrung out. Let the dough sit for two hours.

5. 🛑 Preheat the oven to 350°. When the dough has doubled in size, "punch" it down. Put the dough on the cutting board. With help, divide it into three sections.

Roll one of the sections into a long "snake." Do this with two more of the sections.

6. Put the three rolled sections next to each other on the cutting board. With help, braid the three rolls together. Shape the braid into a ring.

7. 🛑 Ask a grown-up to separate the white from the yellow part of the last egg. Use your fingers to spread the egg yolk over the bread loaf. Sprinkle the poppy seeds on top. 🛑 Bake the bread for 45 minutes.

Hallah is also the traditional bread for the Jewish Sabbath (Saturday). The word "hallah" means "dough" in Hebrew. Some families serve two loaves of Hallah to celebrate God's help when the Jewish people wandered in the desert. Some families believe you shouldn't cut hallah bread with a knife; one should tear a piece off with the fingers. Some Jews believe knives should not be a part of a day that celebrates love.

Apples and Honey

People believe eating this treat on Rosh Hashanah will make the coming year sweet.

You'll need:

apples
honey
hallah bread (See the previous page.)

1. **STOP** Ask a grown-up to help you cut the apples into slices. Be sure to take out the cores.

2. **STOP** With help, cut the bread into pieces.

3. To serve, put the apple slices and the bread onto a plate. Pour the honey into a small bowl.

4. Dip the apples and bread into the honey. Enjoy!

The calendar used in most countries is called the Gregorian calendar. It has 365 days in a year. It is based on the earth's journey around the sun.

The Jewish calendar follows the cycles of the moon. Every month has 29 1/2 days. Each year has 354 days, so every few years an extra month must be added. Otherwise the months would start falling in different seasons.

The Gregorian calendar has been counting for almost 2,000 years. But the Jewish calendar has been counting since Creation, about 6,000 years ago!

Columbus Day
Second Monday in October

In 1492, Christopher Columbus made his first trip to America. His voyage is honored every year on Columbus Day.

Columbus hoped to find a shortcut to Asia for Queen Isabella and King Ferdinand of Spain. He sailed with the ships *Niña*, *Pinta*, and *Santa María*. He was trying to reach lands that were known then as the Indies—India, China, East Indies, and Japan today—by sailing west instead of around Africa. He hoped to find gold, silk, precious stones, and spices.

But Columbus thought the world was smaller than it was. And he thought there was a lot less water and a lot more land. On October 12, 1492, the ships landed on an island in the Caribbean Sea, in what is now the West Indies. On that trip he also sailed into the harbors around present-day Cuba and the Dominican Republic. In addition he had a crash landing on what is now the island of Haiti. He made three more voyages in his lifetime. But Columbus still believed he had reached Asia.

Some people do not think Columbus was a hero. He mistreated the people who lived in the lands he found. He often claimed land for Spain that already belonged to other people. But he was the first European to make lasting contact with land and people in the Western Hemisphere.

In 1792, New York City threw a celebration honoring the 300th anniversary of Columbus's landing. In 1892, President Benjamin Harrison urged the nation to celebrate the 400th anniversary. Celebrations have taken place each year since 1920. Often there are parades and events, and many are sponsored by Italian-American groups. Columbus was born in Italy, so many Italian-Americans celebrate his achievement and their pride on the same day. Columbus Day be-came a national holiday in 1971.

Three Ships

These little boats have sails just like the Niña, the Pinta, and the Santa María.

You'll need:

piece of balsa wood
pencil
small carving knife
chopstick
white construction paper
crayons or markers
scissors
wood glue

1. Draw one of the shapes below on your piece of balsa wood. You can make it as big as you want. **STOP** Ask a grown-up to cut out the shape.

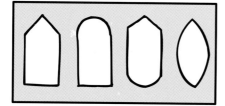

2. Draw one of the sail shapes below on the paper. **STOP** With help, cut out the shape. Color and decorate the sail with the crayons or markers.

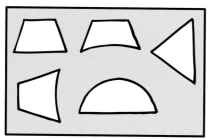

3. Push the chopstick through the sail as shown.

4. Glue the chopstick to the center of the boat. (If your boat is not as long as your chopstick, your grown-up helper may have to cut off some of the chopstick's length.)

 Experiment with your boat. Try different boat sizes. Change the length of the mast (the chopstick). Make the sails bigger and smaller. Which boats sail the best?

Supermarket Scavengers

Find the foods Columbus ate while sailing to the New World!

You'll need:

paper
pencils

1. Each player needs a piece of paper and a pencil.

2. Copy down the following list on the paper:

water	onions
oil	garlic
flour	olives
bacon	rice
salt	sugar
vinegar	honey
chickpeas	cheese
kidney beans	raisins
lentils	almonds

3. Look up and down the aisles of the grocery store to find the foods on this list. When you find one, check it off and write down the aisle number where you found it. The first person to find everything on his list is the winner. Or, the person with the most items checked off when you leave the grocery store is the winner.

 America was named for the Italian explorer Amerigo Vespucci. Vespucci claimed he had made four voyages to the New World beginning in 1497. People believed him because he wrote a letter in 1503 describing what he had seen there. In 1507, a German mapmaker suggested that the new land be called America after Vespucci.

After Vespucci died, people couldn't find any proof that he had sailed in 1497. Over time, Christopher Columbus was given credit for discovering the New World in 1492 (even though he landed on islands and not the mainland).

Halloween
October 31

On Halloween, children dress up in costumes and go door-to-door saying, "Trick or treat!" Before the night is over, they come home with bags full of goodies. Halloween today is a combination of several different new year festivals.

The Celts were people who lived more than 2,000 years ago in what is now England, Scotland, Ireland, and northern France. They celebrated their new year on November 1. On the evening before, they honored their lord of the dead, Samhain. The Celts believed that on this night, Samhain let all the relatives who had died return to their homes on earth.

In 43 A.D., the Romans conquered the Celts. In the fall, the Romans celebrated two festivals. These festivals—Feralia, which honored their dead, and a festival for Pomona, the goddess of fruit and trees—became mixed with the Celts' festival.

In the 800s, after the Christian Church had come along, many of the older festivals were no longer celebrated. But the church made a new holiday called All Saints' Day on November 1.

Trick or Treat

The Mass that was said on this day was called Allhallowmas. The night before All Saints' Day became All Hallows' Eve, which was eventually called All Hallow e'en.

Some of the traditions we follow on Halloween have come from these early festivals. In Ireland, people would march through the streets wearing masks and begging for food during the festival that honored one of their gods, Muck Olla. In England, poor people would go *a-souling* (begging) on All Souls' Day for little treats called soulcakes. Both these customs are a little like trick or treating.

When you carve a face into a pumpkin, you are making a jack-o'-lantern. In England and Ireland, they would carve out beets, potatoes, and turnips. When this custom was brought to America by the immigrants, people started using pumpkins. The legend behind the jack-o'-lantern goes back to Ireland. The Irish said there was a man who died and could not go to heaven because he was selfish. He also could not go to hell because he had played tricks on the devil. This man was named Jack, and he was forced to wander the earth forever carrying a lantern.

Today, many neighborhoods get together for big celebrations that include bonfires, parades, dances, and costume parties.

Bat Mobiles

*Hang these spooky decorations from trees,
on your porch, in the window, or from the ceiling.*

You'll need:

wire coat hanger
black tissue paper
glue
scissors
construction paper

1. STOP Ask a grown-up to gently bend downward both sides of the wire hanger, without changing the shape of the hook or the bottom part.

2. Lay one sheet of the tissue paper on a table. Lay the hanger on one half, so the hook is not on the paper (see below).

3. Squeeze a thin line of glue around the edge of the hanger, as shown below.

4. Fold the other half of the tissue paper up over the hanger. The hanger should now be covered on both sides. Use your hands to press down on top of the paper and hanger to make the glue stick. Let the glue dry overnight.

5. Trim away the extra paper from around the hanger.

6. Cut out four to six tissue-paper strips. Glue two or three strips on each side of your bat to make wings.

7. From the construction paper, cut out eyes, a nose, a mouth, and ears for the bat. Glue them to the tissue paper.

112

Candy Apples

These traditional treats make great party favors or trick-or-treat yummies.

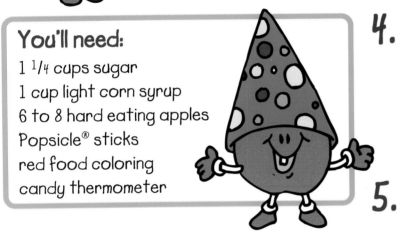

You'll need:

1 1/4 cups sugar
1 cup light corn syrup
6 to 8 hard eating apples
Popsicle® sticks
red food coloring
candy thermometer

1. Mix the sugar and the corn syrup in a heavy saucepan. (STOP) Ask a grown-up to cook the mixture over medium heat.

2. (STOP) Tell your grown-up helper to stir the mixture once in awhile until it starts to boil. (If it looks like the mixture will boil over the top, you can turn the heat down.)

3. (STOP) Ask your helper to attach a candy thermometer to the pot. Be sure the bulb of the thermometer does not touch the sides or bottom of the pot. Let the mixture heat until the thermometer reaches 300˚. (This could take 30 minutes.)

4. While you wait for the mixture to heat, push one Popsicle® stick into the stem end of each apple. Lay a piece of waxed paper on the counter next to the stove.

5. (STOP) When the candy mixture is ready, ask your grown-up helper to take it off the stove. Add the red food coloring until the candy is the color you would like it to be.

6. Dip each apple into the mixture to coat it completely. Place the dipped apple, with the stick facing up, on the waxed paper. Let the apples cool and harden before you eat them.

Quick Costume Ideas

Make one of these quick costumes from stuff you have at home.

King or Queen

A crown made from poster board

A cape made from a large piece of cloth decorated with silver and gold glitter

A scepter made from a wooden spoon covered in foil and decorated

Hobo

Old overalls with patches or holes

Stick with a bandana (stuffed with newspaper) tied to the end of it

Brown makeup streaks to make you look grubby

Black Cat

All black clothes

Mom's black eyeliner to draw whiskers and a nose

A tail made from an old black stocking stuffed with newspaper (attach with a safety pin)

Ghost
An old white sheet with two
eyeholes cut into it

Pirate
Black pants
Black shoes or boots
White long-sleeved shirt
A colorful vest
One clip-on gold hoop earring
A red scarf tied around your head
An eyepatch (optional)
Mom's black eyeliner to
draw a mustache
or beard

Gypsy
Big clip-on gold hoop
earrings
White T-shirt
Long, flowing, colorful
skirt
Colorful shawl

Decorating a Pumpkin

There are lots of ways to decorate a pumpkin besides cutting out shapes with a knife.

The Heidi Pumpkin

Make braids from yellow yarn and use acrylic paint to make a little girl's face.

The Mr. Pumpkinhead

Use pieces of your Mr. Potatohead® and attach them to the pumpkin.

The Veggie Man

Make eyes, ears, a nose, and a mouth out of vegetables, and attach them with toothpicks. For example: cabbage hair, mushroom ears, a carrot nose, and a watermelon mouth.

The Mr. Picassohead

Use the pieces from your Mr. Potatohead®, but put them in crazy places—ears where the nose should be, eyes on top of the head, or a mouth in the back of the head.

The Jack-O'-Pasta

Paint different shapes of pastas in any color you like. When they are dry, paste the pasta shapes on the pumpkin to make a face or designs.

 Other ideas: acrylic paints, felt, pushpins, glitter, Dad's old hat, Con-Tact® paper, construction paper, puffy paint, pinecones, eyes-only mask, party/witch/clown hat, witch nose, fake blood, clown nose, clown hair, pirate patch, fake glasses, cans, paper tubes, plastic bottles, Sunday comics, newspaper (cut or folded), packing peanuts, paper cones, buttons, and small paper plates

On October 29, 1994, in Keene, New Hampshire, 10,540 jack-o'-lanterns were gathered in one place for the Harvest Festival. But none were as big as the giant jack-o'-lantern carved from an 827-pound pumpkin on October 30, 1992. Now that's a lot of pumpkin pies!

Thanksgiving
Fourth Thursday in November

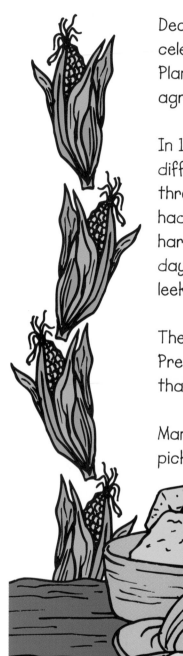

December 4, 1619 was the first time that a day of thanksgiving was celebrated in America. A group of English settlers arrived at Berkeley Plantation in what is now Virginia and gave thanks to God. They agreed that they would give thanks to God every year on that day.

In 1620 and 1621, the settlers in Plymouth, Massachusetts, had a difficult year. After arriving in their new country, they suffered through a horrible winter in which half of their colony died. But they had a fine corn harvest in 1621, and their governor called for a harvest festival to thank God for helping them survive. At this three-day celebration they ate ducks, geese, turkeys, clams, eels, plums, leeks, and corn bread. About 90 Indians joined them for their feast.

The idea of a harvest festival spread to the other colonies. In 1789 President George Washington named November 26 as a day of thanksgiving for that year.

Many states celebrated thanksgiving days, but no one date was picked for the whole country until 1868.

That year President Abraham Lincoln named the last Thursday in November as the official Thanksgiving Day. For 75 years after that, each president did the same every year. Finally, in 1941, Congress ruled that Thanksgiving would be a national holiday and would be observed the fourth Thursday in November.

Most people celebrate Thanksgiving by visiting family and friends and eating a big, special dinner. There is usually turkey, stuffing, mashed potatoes, and vegetables, and for dessert, pumpkin pie. Sometimes there are parades to watch on television. And there are usually lots of football games to watch, too. Some families like to start their celebration by asking each person to tell everyone what they are thankful for.

Table Wreath

*Make this pretty centerpiece to dress
up your family's holiday table.*

You'll need:

Styrofoam® ring
pinecones, dried flowers,
    acorns, colorful leaves,
    nuts (in their shells)
glue
tall, wide candle to stand inside the ring

1. Arrange the pine cones, flowers, acorns, leaves, and nuts on the ring so it is completely covered. Glue the items to the ring.

2. Let the wreath dry completely before you move it or touch it.

3. Place the wreath on the Thanksgiving dinner table and stand the candle in the center of it.

Idea: Instead of a candle, you can stack apples or other fruits in the center of the wreath.

Most Americans celebrate Thanksgiving in November with a big, big meal. But another traditional Thanksgiving celebration has a much smaller selection of foods. Some Pennsylvania Dutch settlers held a thanksgiving service and meal on September 24, 1734, two days after they arrived in Pennsylvania. That special dinner is still celebrated today. The traditional spread consists of water, bread, butter, and apple-butter.

120

Corn Bread Squares

This delicious bread is like a kind of bread served at the first Thanksgiving.

You'll need:

1 cup yellow cornmeal
1 cup unsifted flour
4 1/4 teaspoons baking powder
1/4 teaspoon salt
2 1/2 tablespoons sugar
1/3 cup margarine
1 cup milk
2 eggs

1. In a large bowl, combine the cornmeal, flour, baking powder, salt, and sugar.

2. (STOP) With a grown-up's help, blend in the margarine using an electric mixer.

3. In a small bowl, whisk together the milk and eggs. Pour this mixture into the cornmeal bowl, and briskly stir for a few minutes.

4. Grease an 8-inch square baking dish. Pour the batter into the dish.

5. (STOP) Ask a grown-up to bake the bread at 425° for 20 to 25 minutes.

6. Let the corn bread cool. Cut it into squares. If you are not serving it immediately, refrigerate the bread.

Native American Game

*This game is typical of the kinds of games played
by Native American children long ago.*

For 2 or more players

You'll need:

10 small pebbles
small basket
black marker
paper
pencil

1. Draw a black dot on one side of each pebble.

2. Place the pebbles in the basket. Taking turns, each player shakes the bowl and pours the pebbles on the floor.

3. Players get one point for each pebble that has its black dot faceup.

4. The first player to reach 50 points wins the game.

Cornhusk Dolls

Pilgrim children made these dolls from leftover cornhusks.

You'll need:

pencil
tracing paper
scissors
cardboard
9 pieces of cornhusk
plant mister
tacky glue
Spanish moss
ribbon scraps
paper towels
markers or paints

1. Trace the doll pattern on page 155 onto the tracing paper. Cut it out.

2. Trace around the tracing-paper cutout onto the cardboard. Cut out the pattern from the cardboard.

3. Lay a few paper towels on a table. Lightly mist both sides of all the cornhusks with water. Lay them on the paper towels. Let them sit for about five minutes.

4. Take one husk and loop it from front to back over the top of the doll frame as shown. Glue it in place.

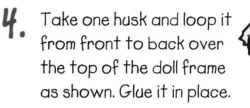

5. Loop a cornhusk around each arm. Glue them in place.

6. Glue the straight ends of the remaining cornhusks to the doll's waist. Let the glue dry completely.

7. To finish, glue Spanish moss to the head for hair. Tie a ribbon around the center of the doll. Draw a face.

Sweet Potato Pudding

Sweet potatoes aren't just for dinnertime—try them in this anytime dessert. For some families sweet potatoes are a traditional Thanksgiving food

You'll need:

4 medium eggs, slightly beaten
4 cups canned sweet potatoes
1 cup brown sugar or honey
12 ounces evaporated milk
1 1/2 teaspoons cinnamon
1 teaspoon salt
1 teaspoon ginger
1/2 teaspoon ground cloves
marshmallows
butter

1. Combine all the ingredients except the marshmallows. Mix well.

2. Rub butter around the inside of a baking dish. Pour the sweet potato mixture into the dish.

3. STOP Ask a grown-up to bake the pudding in a 350° oven for 45 minutes to one hour. (When your helper inserts a tooth-pick or knife into the pudding, it should come out clean.)

4. Drop marshmallows on top of the pudding. STOP Place the dish back in the oven until the marshmallows are browned. Let the pudding cool. Serve with graham crackers.

Basket Stix

This game is a lot like one of the most popular Native American games of chance.

You'll need:
5 Popsicle® sticks
markers or crayons
shoebox
25 toothpicks for each player

2 moons and 3 uncolored sides =
  10 toothpicks from each player

2 stars and 3 black sides =
  10 toothpicks from each player

1 moon, 1 star, and 3 uncolored sides =
  1 toothpick from each player

1 moon, 1 star, and 3 black sides =
  1 toothpick from each player

1. On one of the Popsicle® sticks, draw a star on one side. Draw a crescent moon on the other side. Do this with a second stick.

2. On the last three sticks, color one side of each black. Place all five sticks in the shoebox.

3. To play, give each player 25 toothpicks. Take turns tossing the Popsicle® sticks out of the shoebox and onto a table.

4. When you throw the sticks, you take a certain number of toothpicks from each player depending on how the sticks land.

Any other combination does not earn you any toothpicks.

For example, if you toss the sticks and one stick lands with its moon side facing up, one lands with its star side facing up, and the last three land with their black sides facing up, then you take one toothpick from each player. If you get one moon facing up, one star facing up, one black side facing up, and two uncolored sides facing up, you get no toothpicks from the other players.

5. The game continues until one of the players runs out of toothpicks. The remaining players count how many toothpicks they have. The winner is the player with the most toothpicks.

125

Hanukkah
Eight Days, Usually in December

Hanukkah celebrates the miracle of a great Jewish victory. It is also called the Festival of Lights or the Festival of Dedication.

About 2,400 years ago, the influence of the ancient Greeks was spreading to other parts of the world. It reached Israel, where the Jews lived, but many were not interested. They did not believe in the many gods that the Greeks did. They believed in their one God.

Then, Antiochus IV, a Syrian king, demanded that all the Jews follow the Greek ways, and give up their one God. He made laws that the Jews could not celebrate their holidays. He burned their books. He killed people when they would not worship the Greek god, Zeus. He even went to the only Jewish Temple in the world and made an altar to Zeus there.

The Jews were not frightened, and they would not give up their God. A small group of Jews, called the Maccabees (which means "hammers"), fought the Syrians with farm tools and sticks. Somehow, through a miracle, they were able to beat the Syrians. If they hadn't, it would have been the end of the Jewish people and their religion.

After they won, they went to their Temple to praise God. But when they got there, they found the Temple dirty, filled with statues of the Greek gods. They wanted to light their menorah, but they only had a little bit of oil. The *menorah* was an oil lamp that was supposed to be lighted all the time. The Jews thought the bit of oil would only keep the menorah lit for a day. But the lamp kept burning, day after day, for eight days.

Today, Jews light their menorahs for eight nights. There are nine candles on a Hanukkah menorah. Eight candles stand for the nights that the oil burned in the Temple. The ninth candle is the *shammash*, which is used to light all the others. Jewish families light the candles at sundown.

Other traditions on Hanukkah include eating *latkes* (potato pancakes), giving gold foil-covered chocolate "coins," and playing the *dreidel* game. Many families exchange small gifts on each night of Hanukkah.

Homemade Hanukkah Menorah

Light one candle for each night of Hanukkah.
On the first night, light one. On the second night, light two, and so on.

You'll need:

9 blue birthday-cake candles
11 white LifeSavers®
1-inch by 8-inch strip of
    poster board
glue
1 white Certs® candy

1. Spread a thick coat of glue down the center of the poster board.

2. Glue nine LifeSavers® in a row onto the poster board. Glue four LifeSavers® on the left side of the strip and four on the right side. Glue the Certs® candy in the center.

3. Glue another LifeSavers® on top of each piece of candy on the bottom row. Glue a third LifeSavers® on top of the center stack. Let the glue dry completely.

🛑 *Do not light the menorah candles without a grown-up's help!*

4. Set one candle in the hole of each candy piece.

How to light a traditional menorah:

1. The first candle is placed in the branch that is all the way to the right. As candles are added, they are placed in branches to the left of the candles that are already in the menorah.

2. Light the candles at sundown. Start with the candle furthest on the left and move toward the last candle on the right.

3. On the first night, light one candle. On the second night, light two candles. Add a candle each night.

4. The candles must stay lighted for at least at 30 minutes. Most families keep them lighted until they burn down and use new candles each night.

Latkes

Latkes are also called potato pancakes. They are fried in oil and remind Jewish families of the tiny jug of oil that lasted for eight days.

Makes 24 small latkes

You'll need:

4 large potatoes, peeled and grated
$1/4$ onion, chopped
2 eggs
$1/4$ cup flour
1 teaspoon salt
$1/4$ teaspoon pepper
$1/4$ teaspoon baking powder
oil
applesauce

1. In a large bowl, stir together the potatoes, onion, and eggs until they are mixed well.

2. Add the flour, salt, pepper, and baking powder. Stir to mix well.

3. STOP Ask a grown-up to heat $1/2$ cup of oil in a skillet.

4. STOP Tell your grown-up helper to drop spoonfuls of the mixture into the hot oil. Then flatten each spoonful with a spoon to make pancakes.

5. STOP Cook about three minutes on each side, until the pancakes are browned. Ask your helper to drain the latkes on paper towels.

6. Serve the latkes with applesauce.

Dreidel Game

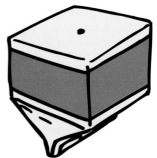

The Hebrew letters on a dreidel stand for
"Nes gadol hayah sham," which means
"A great miracle happened there."

You'll need:

pint-sized milk or cream carton
tape
unsharpened pencil
white construction paper
black marker
tracing paper
pencil
scissors
pennies, nuts, beans, small
   candies (such as *Gummy* bears
   or M&Ms®)

To make the dreidel:

1. Open the top of the milk carton as shown. Rinse it out, and let it dry completely.

2. Tape the top closed, leaving a small opening in the center, big enough for a pencil to fit through.

3. (STOP) Ask a grown-up to make a small hole in the center of the carton bottom, using the points of the scissors.

4. Slide the pencil through the openings at the top and bottom. The eraser should be at the top of the carton, and the unsharpened end at the bottom.

5. Cover the sides of the carton by gluing on squares of white construction paper.

6. Use the black marker to trace the Hebrew letters shown on the next page onto the tracing paper.

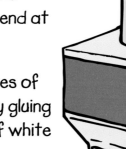

7. (STOP) Cut out the squares with the Hebrew letters from the tracing paper. Glue one on each side of the milk carton. Now you've made your dreidel!

To play the dreidel game:

1. Each player starts with an equal number of small candies, pennies, or other markers.

2. At the beginning of the game, each player puts one piece into the center of the playing area. This is the "pot."

3. Decide how many rounds will be played—how many times will each player get to spin before the game is over?

4. Players take turns spinning the dreidel. When the dreidel finishes spinning, the player follows the direction for the symbol on the dreidel. See the symbols below. The next player on the left then takes his turn.

5. When the pot is empty, every player puts one item in the pot again.

6. The player with the most markers at the end of the game wins.

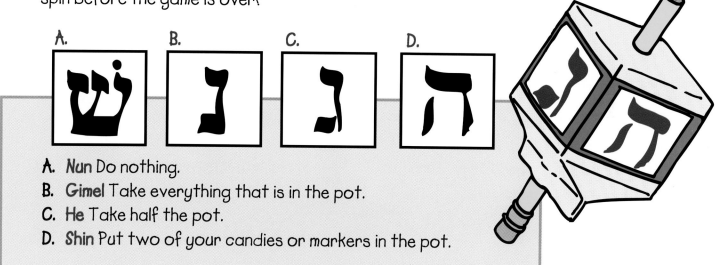

A.   B.   C.   D.

A. *Nun* Do nothing.
B. *Gimel* Take everything that is in the pot.
C. *He* Take half the pot.
D. *Shin* Put two of your candies or markers in the pot.

Antiochus made laws that forbade Jewish people from reading the Torah (the Jewish Bible. Jewish families had to find a way to hide what they were doing. Some children secretly memorized the Torah. They would study together in groups. When they heard the footsteps of Antiochus's soldiers coming, they would pull out tops and pretend they were playing. That was the start of the dreidel game.

Sufganiyyot

*Jewish families in Israel celebrate Hanukkah
by making and eating these orange donuts.*

Makes 9 donuts

You'll need:

1/3 cup plus 2 teaspoons orange juice
1/2 stick margarine, melted
2 tablespoons granulated sugar
1 package dry yeast
1 1/2 cups flour
1 egg, beaten
dash of salt
powdered sugar

1. In a saucepan, stir together the orange juice, margarine, and granulated sugar. (STOP) Ask a grown-up to heat the mixture until it is lukewarm.

2. Stir the yeast into the juice mixture until it dissolves.

3. Add the flour, eggs, and salt to the saucepan. Mix well, until it is a smooth dough.

4. Sprinkle some flour onto a cutting board.

5. Knead the dough for a few minutes.

6. Rub some butter onto the inside of a medium-sized bowl. Place the dough in the bowl. Cover the bowl with a towel. Let the dough rise for 30 minutes.

7. Knead the dough again. Shape the dough into donuts. Let them stand for another 30 minutes.

8. (STOP) Ask a grown-up to heat 2 inches of oil in a large frying pan. Ask your helper to fry the donuts until they are golden brown on both sides. Drain the donuts on paper towels.

9. Sprinkle the powdered sugar on top.

Hanukkah Card

Wish your friends and family a happy Hanukkah with this special dreidel card.

You'll need:

2 same-sized card envelopes (If you use white, color them with a marker.)

construction paper

silver glitter

glue

black marker

scissors

1. Lay the envelopes on the table so the flaps are open and the back of the envelopes are facing you. Spread glue along the sides and flaps and glue the two envelopes together.

2. 🛑 Cut a 8-inch strip of paper from the construction paper. This will be the dreidel handle.

3. On one end of the strip, write PULL. On the other end of the strip, write Happy Hanukkah! and sign your name. Place the strip inside the pocket of the card so the end that says PULL is sticking out.

> Happy Hanukkah!   PULL

4. Draw one of the Hebrew letters from page 131 on one side of the card. Draw a different Hebrew letter on the other side.

5. Spread some glue along the edges of the card and handle. Sprinkle with glitter. Let dry.

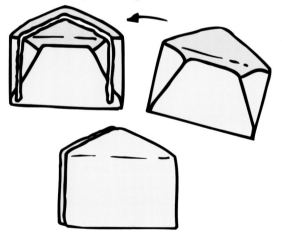

Christmas
December 25

Christians celebrate the birth of Jesus on Christmas. It is a very exciting time of year, loved by kids and grown-ups alike.

During the Christmas season, stores and houses are decorated in red and green. People decorate Christmas trees with bright, shiny ornaments, candy canes, cranberry and popcorn strings, lights, and tinsel. Families bake Christmas cookies and whip up other special treats in the kitchen. It is a great time for visiting your friends, and often little gifts are exchanged. There is lots of music and singing, and many people throw parties. People send Christmas cards to one another. On Christmas Eve and Christmas Day, many families go to church.

Many of the customs that we follow today started a long time ago at some early festivals. During the year-end celebrations of the ancient Romans and Europeans, people exchanged gifts.

134

Today we eat lots of special foods at this time of year, just like they did at the first Christmas celebrations (except they ate things like roasted boars and peacocks!).

The Christmas trees we put up today were probably inspired by the "paradise tree" in Germany. A play about Adam and Eve was performed each year on December 24 in medieval Germany. In the play, one of the props was an evergreen tree with apples hanging on it. The German people began decorating their homes with trees like this, and adding other fruits, candles, and paper flowers to the decorations. When the German settlers came to Pennsylvania, they brought this custom of decorating trees to America.

Evergreen trees are trees that do not lose their leaves or die during the winter. People used them as year-end decorations to remind themselves that they could overcome the harshness of winter. When they were made part of the Christmas decorations, it reminded Christians that Jesus gave them eternal life.

Christmas is a very religious holiday. But most importantly, it is a time to show your family and friends that you love them.

Snowballs

This frozen treat is a yummy dessert for Christmas, or any time of the year.

You'll need:

vanilla ice cream
shredded coconut
maraschino cherries

1. Let the ice cream sit for a few minutes to soften it a bit.

2. Lay a piece of waxed paper on the table. Pour the shredded coconut onto the waxed paper.

3. Scoop out a round ball of ice cream. Place it on top of the coconut on the waxed paper.

4. Roll the ice-cream ball around in the coconut until it is completely covered.

5. Continue until you've used all the ice cream and coconut.

6. Wrap each ball in plastic wrap. Place the balls in a container. Freeze them until they are solid again.

7. Place a cherry on top when you serve the snowballs.

No-Cook Fudge

A batch of fudge makes a great Christmas present for anyone!

You'll need:

1/4 cup butter
1/4 cup sweetened condensed milk
1 teaspoon vanilla
1 pound confectioners' sugar
3/4 cup cocoa
1/4 teaspoon salt

1. STOP Ask a grown-up to melt the butter in the microwave (try it on high for ten seconds).

2. Stir in the milk and vanilla.

3. In another bowl, mix together the sugar, cocoa, and salt.

4. Add the sugar mixture, a little at a time, to the milk mixture. Mix well until it is creamy and smooth.

5. Grease the inside of a pan. Pour the mixture into the pan. Chill in the refrigerator until it is solid. Cut into squares.

Mini "Gingerbread" House

*Use these tiny houses as placecards at the dinner table,
or as decorations under or on the tree.
Or give them as gifts to your friends.*

You'll need:

1 egg white
1½ cups powdered sugar
empty half-pint milk carton
assorted candies for decoration (mini
    candy canes, licorice, LifeSavers®,
    M&M's®, Skittles®, Hershey's Kisses®,
    gumdrops, and others)
6 graham-cracker squares

1. Mix together the egg white and powdered sugar to make frosting.

2. Spread some frosting on one side each of four graham-cracker squares. Press each square onto one side of the milk carton. Spread more frosting over the edges where the crackers meet to hold the walls together.

3. To make a roof, dip one edge of each remaining graham-cracker square in the frosting. Press the edges together at an angle to make a roof shape, as shown here. Let the roof harden so it stays together.

4. To attach the roof to the house, spread some frosting along the top edge of the crackers that are already attached to the carton on the sides with the slanted tops (see below). Rest the roof on top of the carton. Press the edges gently against the frosted edges of the other crackers.

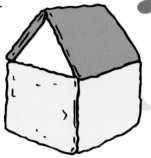

5. Decorate the house with the candy. Use the frosting to "glue" the candies to the roof and sides of the house.

On December 2, 1988, a giant gingerbread house was built by 102 volunteers in Des Moines, Iowa. The house was 52 feet high and 32 feet square and was made of 2,000 sheets of gingerbread and 1,650 pounds of icing!

Yule-Log Cake

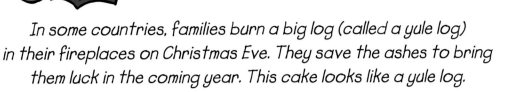

In some countries, families burn a big log (called a yule log) in their fireplaces on Christmas Eve. They save the ashes to bring them luck in the coming year. This cake looks like a yule log.

Makes 2 yule logs

You'll need:

1 box chocolate cake mix
4 eggs
¹/₂ cup water
cocoa
12-ounce container of Cool Whip®

1. (STOP) With a grown-up's help, beat the eggs with an electric mixer on high speed for five minutes.

2. Add the water and cake mix to the eggs. (STOP) Beat on low speed until the cake mix is moist.

3. Spray a jelly-roll pan with nonstick cooking spray. Line the pan with waxed paper. Spray the waxed paper with nonstick cooking spray.

4. Pour half the cake batter into the pan. Spread evenly to make a thin layer.

5. (STOP) Bake the cake at 350° for about 13 minutes.

6. Lay a clean cloth towel on the table. With help, spread four tablespoons of the cocoa onto the towel to form a 10-inch by 15-inch rectangle.

7. While the cake is still very warm, loosen the edges from the pan. (STOP) Ask your grown-up helper to turn the cake out onto the cocoa-dusted towel. Peel off the waxed paper.

8. Starting at the narrow end, roll the cake and towel together. Let the cake cool completely.

9. Gently unroll the cake. Spread the Cool Whip® over the cake. Roll it up again without the towel.

10. Repeat steps 4 through 9 with the rest of the batter to make a second yule log.

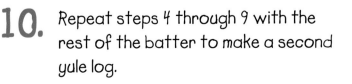

Clay Ornaments

You can shape your own Christmas-tree ornaments with this easy-to-bake clay.

You'll need:

1 1/2 cups water
2 cups salt
1 cup cornstarch
Christmas cookie cutters
acrylic paint, glue, glitter, buttons,
    fabric scraps
string or ribbon

1. **STOP** Ask a grown-up to bring the water to a boil.

2. **STOP** Take the saucepan off the stove. Stir in the salt and cornstarch.

3. **STOP** Now heat the mixture on low. Cook the dough until it is hard to stir.

4. Pour the dough onto waxed paper. Let it cool.

5. Knead the dough. Use a rolling pin to roll out the dough until it is 1/8-inch thick.

6. Use the cookie cutters to cut out Christmas shapes from the dough.

7. Use a toothpick to poke a hole at the top of each shape. Let the dough shapes dry for a few days.

8. Paint and decorate the ornaments.

9. Thread lengths of string or ribbon through each hole and tie the ends together to make hangers for your ornaments.

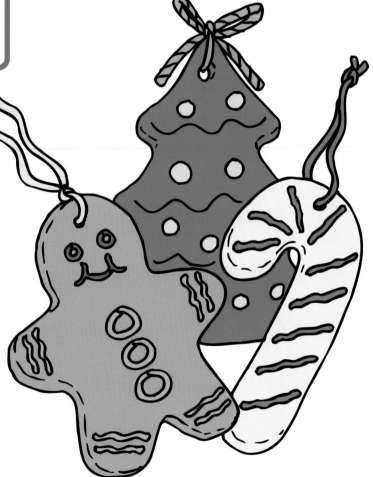

The tallest Christmas tree was put up in 1950 at the Northgate Shopping Center in Seattle, Washington. The tree was a Douglas fir that stood 221 feet tall!

Handmade Christmas Wreath

These wreaths make great gifts or decorations.

You'll need:

large brown paper bag
three yards of one-inch-wide fabric
    ribbon
small holiday figures or ornaments
scissors
stapler or tape
pipe cleaner
glue

1. Cut the paper bag down one side. Cut out the bottom of the bag, as shown.

Cut.   Cut.

2. Spread the bag out flat. Roll the bag from the longer side.

3. Staple or tape the ends of the roll together to make a circle shape.

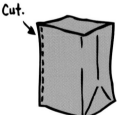

4. Wrap the one-inch ribbon around the wreath as shown . Glue or tie the ends down.

5. Use the rest of the ribbon to make a bow. If you don't know how, ask a grown-up to help. Glue the bow to the wreath.

6. Glue the figures and ornaments onto the wreath to decorate it.

7. Wrap the pipe cleaner around the top of the wreath for hanging.

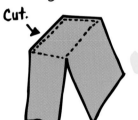

Gift Wrap Ideas

Try some of these easy and inexpensive ideas for wrapping presents.

Place the gift in a brown paper bag that you have decorated with markers, crayons, paints, and glitter. Use ribbon to tie the top closed.

Wrap small gifts in colored tissue paper. Place the tissue paper in a small plastic bag so the tissue paper sticks out of the top. Tie with yarn.

Wrap a box with aluminum foil. Tie yarn around it and make a bow. You can draw on the foil with permanent markers.

Hide the gift. Write out clues to help the person find the gift. Hide that clue. Write out a clue to help the person find that clue, and on and on. You can have many clues. Hide them and have them lead from one to another.

Over the sofa and through the hall, then six inches to the left of the soccer ball.

Cover a box with different colors of construction paper.

Marzipan

This sweet is popular in Germany at Christmas.

You'll need:

8 ounces almond paste
1/4 cup corn syrup
3/4 cup marshmallow creme
1 pound confectioners' sugar
food coloring dissolved in water
paintbrush

1. Mix the almond paste, corn syrup, marshmallow creme, and sugar together with your hands until it is well-blended.

2. Form the marzipan into shapes of ornaments, toys, animals, and other favorite things.

3. Paint the shapes with food coloring.

You can stick Popsicle® sticks in your creations to make marzipan lollipops.

Kwanzaa
December 26 through January 1

Kwanzaa celebrates the African-American experience and people, but anyone can celebrate this holiday.

Kwanzaa was created by Dr. Maulana Karenga in 1966. He wanted to create a holiday that would bring together the African-American people. He got the idea for Kwanzaa from the "first fruit" festivals that were held in Africa. The word *kwanzaa* comes from the Swahili words for "first fruit."

Each night during Kwanzaa, a candle is lit in a special candleholder called a *kinara*. The family talks about the special principle for that day, and what they can do to carry it out. Sometimes people may exchange gifts at Kwanzaa. The gifts are usually handmade and have special meaning to the African-American people. Gift ideas include jewelry, music makers, clothing, and toys.

Near the end of Kwanzaa, there is a special meal called the *karamu*. Families usually serve foods inspired by African dishes like beans and greens, sweet potatoes, roasts, corn bread, and sweets. There is music, dancing, and singing.

There are seven principles of Kwanzaa. One is honored on each day during the celebration. The seven principles, or *Nguzo Saba*, are:

Umoja (oo-MOH-jah) –Unity. This means you work together with other people you know.

Kujichagulia (koo-jee-chah-goo-LEE-ah)–Self-determination. This means you are responsible for what happens in your life.

Ujima (oo-JEE-mah)–Collective work and responsibility. You should help others when they need it.

Ujamaa (oo-jah-MAH)–Collective economics. This means African-Americans should help African-American stores and businesses succeed.

Nia (NEE-ah)–Purpose. This means African-Americans should work to restore the African-American community to its traditional greatness.

Kuumba (koo-OOM-bah)–Creativity. Use your imagination to make your community a better place.

Imani (ee-MAH-nee)–Faith. This means to believe in our people, our parents, our teachers, our leaders, and the African-American struggle.

You may think that these principles are too hard for you. You may think you are too young or too small. Or maybe you think that because you are not African-American, you don't have to worry about it. Everyone can work toward these goals. You can have ideas, make plans, and tell other people about them.

Peanut Stew

In Africa, peanuts are called groundnuts. This dish reminds us of the traditional foods eaten by native Africans.

Makes 4 servings

You'll need:

3 pounds of chicken, rinsed
1 inch of fresh ginger
1 cup chopped onion
2 cups water
1 medium tomato, chopped
2/3 cup crunchy peanut butter
2 tablespoons tomato paste
2 teaspoons salt
1 teaspoon ground black pepper
2 tablespoons cayenne pepper

1. (STOP) Ask a grown-up to cut the chicken into cubes.

2. Place the chicken, ginger, onion, tomato, and water in a large saucepan. (STOP) Cover the pot, and bring the mixture to a boil. Once the mixture boils, turn the heat down a bit. Let the pot simmer for one hour.

3. Place the peanut butter in a bowl. (STOP) Ask a grown-up to put some of the liquid from the chicken mixture in the bowl also. Blend the peanut butter and chicken mixture together. Pour the peanut butter/chicken mixture back into the chicken mixture in the saucepan.

4. Add the tomato paste, salt, and peppers. (STOP) Ask your grown-up helper to partially cover the saucepan. Simmer the stew on low heat for 30 minutes more, so the chicken is tender.

Mazao Bowl

Fill this bowl with fruits and vegetables. Those foods represent the traditional harvest festival and the importance of working together.

You'll need:

large plastic bowl
plastic bag
paper towels
thin paste (or mix white glue with water)
scrap paper torn into strips
scissors
acrylic paints
shellac

1. Line the inside of the bowl with the plastic bag. Wet a paper towel. Lay it in the bowl, on top of the plastic. Be sure the bowl is completely lined with wet paper towels (use more than one if you need to).

2. One by one, dip the paper strips completely in the paste. Lay each strip in the bowl. Press the strip against the bowl so it sticks and it is flat. Continue until the papier-mâché bowl is about 3/4 inch thick. Be sure the bottom of the bowl is flat so it will sit properly on the table. Let the bowl dry overnight.

3. Pull the plastic away from the papier-mâché bowl.

4. STOP With a grown-up's help, cut around the edge of the bowl to make it even.

5. Paint the bowl with acrylic paints. Let the bowl dry completely. Coat the inside and outside of the bowl with shellac and let dry.

Wet paper towel

Plastic bag

Kinara

The kinara symbolizes all the generations of African ancestors. Each candle stands for one of the principles of Kwanzaa.

You'll need:

sanded piece of wood, 1 inch high, 4 inches wide, and 15 inches long
wood glue or glue gun
8 wooden blocks (plain or with letters that spell out Kwanzaa)
hammer
8 to 10 nails
black, gold, red, or green paint
3 green candles
3 red candles
1 black candle
knife

1. Place the wooden blocks on the piece of wood. Leave spaces between the blocks that are slightly smaller than the width of the bottom of the candles, as shown below.

2. Glue the blocks to the board. Let the glue dry.

3. STOP Ask a grown-up to nail the blocks to the underside of the board.

4. Paint the board, being careful not to paint over the blocks if they have letters on them. Let the board dry overnight.

5. STOP Ask a grown-up to use the knife to cut the sides of the candle bottoms so they fit snugly between the blocks.

6. Place the candles between the blocks—three green on the right, three red on the left, and the black one in the center.

Celebrating Birthdays

Everybody has a birthday to celebrate. And there are lots of ways to do it.

Make a birthday cake. Make a special card. Draw a picture. Make a scrapbook. Throw a surprise party. Make a present. Have a picnic.

Birthdays are fun holidays because they are your very own special celebration. They are great times to think about how you have changed since your last birthday. You can also make a list of things you would like to do before your next birthday. Sometimes it's fun to look at old pictures with your family.

Whatever you do on your birthday, make a special memory. This is *your* special day.

Chocolate Birthday Cake

Everyone loves birthday cake! This cake takes a little work, but it's worth it!

You'll need:

2 cups cake flour
2 teaspoons baking powder
1/2 teaspoon baking soda
1/4 teaspoon salt
1/2 cup plus 2 tablespoons cocoa
1 1/2 cups granulated sugar
1/2 cup plus 2 tablespoons margarine
1/2 cup warm water
2/3 cup milk
2 eggs
1 teaspoon vanilla extract
whipped topping or frosting

1. (STOP) Ask a grown-up to preheat the oven to 350°.

2. Combine the flour, baking powder, baking soda, salt, cocoa, and sugar. Add the margarine, water, milk, eggs, and vanilla.

3. (STOP) Ask a grown-up to use an electric mixer to blend the ingredients on very low speed until they are mixed completely. Then mix on medium speed for three minutes.

4. Rub some margarine or butter onto the bottoms and sides of the insides of two 9-inch layer cake pans. Pour the cake batter into the pans. (STOP) Bake for 30 minutes.

5. Let the layers cool for ten minutes. (STOP) Ask a grown-up to remove the layers from the pans. Let the layers cool completely before you frost them. If you are using whipped topping, don't top the cake until right before you are ready to serve it. Frost the top and sides of one layer. Put the second layer on top. Frost the top and sides of the second layer.

The largest birthday cake ever made was created to celebrate the 100th birthday of Fort Payne, Alabama. The cake was shaped like the state of Alabama. It weighed more than 128,238 pounds, including 16,209 pounds of icing!

Cake Decorating

*Try some of these ideas the next time
you bake a birthday cake.*

Doll Cake

Bake the cake in a bowl. Turn it
upside down to make a skirt. Dig out
a hole in the middle and
stand a Barbie® in the
hole. Decorate the
cake like her
skirt.

Mini Clown Cakes

Bake cupcakes. Use
upside down ice-cream
cones as hats.
Decorate with
frosting and
small candies.

Hamburger Cake

Bake one white layer and one
chocolate layer in regular round cake
pans. Bake another white layer in a
bowl. Stack the layers so the rounded
layer is on the top and looks like a roll.
The chocolate layer should be in the
middle. Decorate with white frosting
tinted red, yellow, and green (above
and below the chocolate layer). Frost
the top and edges of the bottom with
yellow-tinted frosting. Toss on some
yellow sprinkles. Use candies or
frosting to make a face on top if you
want.

Fuzzy-Wuzzy Cake

Bake the cake in two bowls, one
smaller than the other. Sit them next to
each other so they make a head and body.
Decorate like your favorite animal. Use
Twinkies®, lady fingers, or cookies to make
legs and a tail. Color coconut with food
coloring to
make the fur.
What else
would you
add?

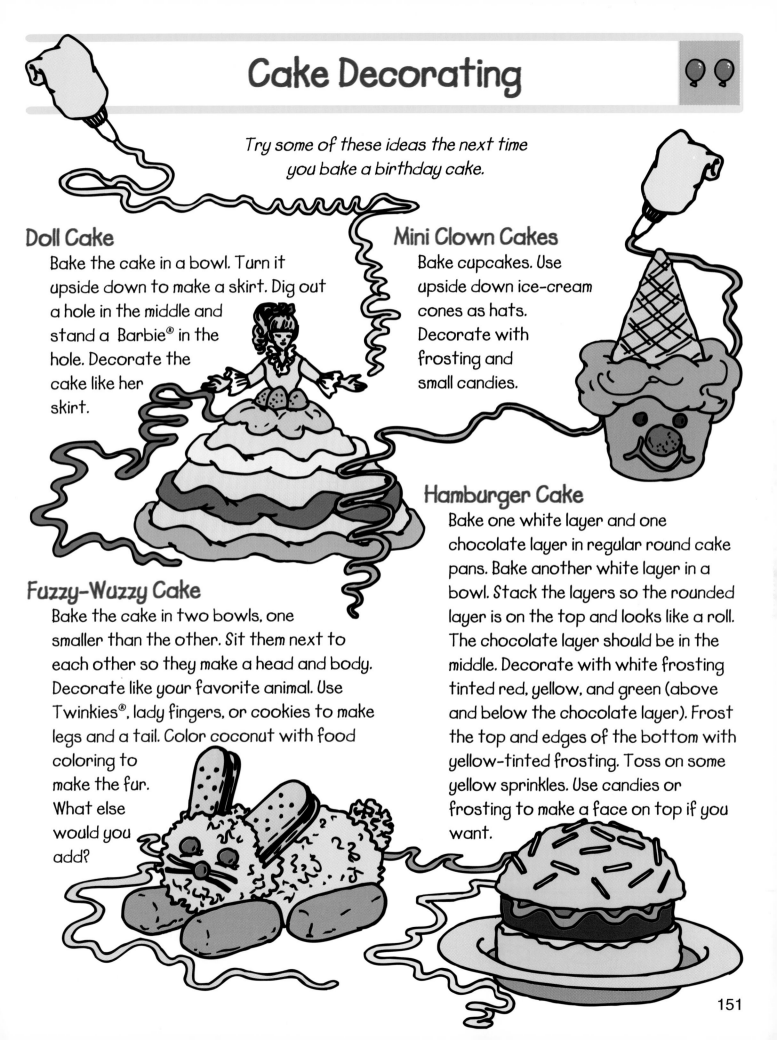

Ready-to-Eat Candleholders

These yummy candleholders are easy to make and delicious to eat.

You'll need:

1/3 cup corn syrup

1/2 teaspoon salt

1 pound powdered sugar

1/3 cup margarine (softened)

1 teaspoon flavoring (vanilla, banana, almond, or another extract)

food coloring

small paper or plastic cups

cornstarch (optional)

1. Place the powdered sugar in a bowl.

2. Add the corn syrup, salt, and margarine. Stir with a spoon until it is mixed well. Add more powdered sugar or some cornstarch if the mixture is too sticky. (The mixture should not stick to your hands.) Now you have made a clay mixture.

3. Put a bit of the clay mixture in a paper cup. Use one paper cup for each color of clay you want to make. Add the flavoring and coloring to each cup. Mix the clay with your fingers or a spoon until it is evenly colored.

4. Take the clay out of the cup and roll it into balls. Mold the clay into the shapes you want for your candleholders. Press the bottom of one candle into each holder. Place the candleholders on the frosted cake. You can also shape the candy clay balls into flowers and other fun shapes to decorate the cake.

5. When you are done with the candles, remove them from the holders. Remove any melted wax from the candleholders. Now they are ready to eat!

Birthday Book

This book makes a wonderful gift full of memories for a friend or relative.

You'll need:

12 sheets of 9-inch by 12-inch construction paper
glue
stapler
marker
photographs of the birthday person

1. Fold each sheet of construction paper in half. Glue the 6-inch sides of each piece together. Now you've made 12 pockets.

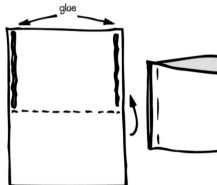

glue

2. Stack the 12 pockets together. 🛑 With help, staple the pockets together on the left side to make a book. The pocket openings should be on top.

3. Label each pocket with a marker. You can label each with different years or ages (for example, 1990 or 5 years old), or with different topics (for example, birthday parties, vacations, Christmas, friends, and others).

4. Place the photos or other mementos (like ticket stubs, letters, cards, and other items) in the pockets.

Joshua's Birthday Book
Age 5

Or try this:
Parents and grandparents love to get birthday books about YOU! So fill the pockets with pictures of yourself and artwork you have done.

153

Chocolate Candy Apples

These yummy treats are terrific party snacks or favors.

You'll need:

6 apples

1/4 cup margarine

1 ounce unsweetened chocolate

1 cup brown sugar

1/2 cup light corn syrup

7 ounces sweetened condensed milk

1/2 teaspoon vanilla

1 cup crushed candy bar (like Heath®, Skor®, or Butterfinger®), sprinkles, coconut, or chopped nuts

6 Popsicle® sticks

candy thermometer

ribbon or yarn (optional)

1. Pull the stems from the apples. Press one Popsicle® stick into each apple where the stem was attached.

2. STOP Ask a grown-up to melt the margarine and chocolate over low heat.

3. STOP With help, add the sugar, corn syrup, and milk. Stir well. Place the candy thermometer in the mixture. Cook the mixture over medium heat, stirring often.

4. STOP When the candy thermometer reaches 245°, remove the mixture from the heat. Add the vanilla.

5. Dip each apple into the chocolate so it is completely covered. Roll the chocolate-covered apple in the crushed candy, sprinkles, nuts, etc. Stand the apples on waxed paper so the stick is pointing up. Let them cool for 30 minutes.

6. If you are not serving the apples immediately, wrap each one in waxed paper and tie closed with ribbon or yarn.

Cornhusk Doll Pattern

INDEX

INDEX

INDEX

INDEX

INDEX

For Julia and Joey

©1997 by THE EDUCATION CENTER, INC.
All rights reserved except as noted below.

Library of Congress Cataloging-in-Publication Data

Staino, Patricia A., 1970–
    Holidays & celebrations with your kids / written by Patricia A. Staino ;
illustrated by Marilynn G. Barr.
        p.   cm. — (Magic moments)
    Includes index.
    Summary: Provides descriptions of a variety of year-round holidays as well as projects
and activities to celebrate them, from New Year's Eve and Valentine's Day to Groundhog
Day and May Day.
    ISBN 1-56234-192-8 (pbk.)
    1. Holidays—Juvenile literature.   2. Holiday decorations—Juvenile literature.
3. Holiday cookery—Juvenile literature.   4. Festivals—Juvenile literature.   [1. Holidays.
2. Festivals. 3. Holiday decorations. 4. Holiday cookery. 5. Handicraft. 6. Cookery.]
I. Barr, Marilynn G., ill.   II. Title.   III. Title: Holidays & celebrations with your kids.
IV. Series: Magic moments (Greensboro, N.C.)
GT3933.S68   1997
394.26—dc21   97-38315
                                                                            CIP
                                                                            AC

Cover Illustration by Marilynn Grant Barr

The Education Center, Inc.
P. O. Box 9753
Greensboro, NC 27429-0753
http://www.theeducationcenter.com

Manufactured in the United States
10 9 8 7 6 5 4 3 2 1 0

Magic Moments™

Holidays & Celebrations With Your Kids

Written by Patricia A. Staino
Illustrated by Marilynn G. Barr

The Education Center, Inc.
Greensboro, North Carolina